LETTERS AND SOUNDS:

Principles and Practice of High Quality Phonics

To purchase a copy please visit:

www.TheNationalCurriculum.com

or scan this code to take you there:

Corporate Author: The Department For Education

Published by: Shurville Publishing

ISBN: 9780992834159

Letters and Sounds:

Principles and Practice of High Quality Phonics

Primary
National Strategy

department for
education and skills

Creating Opportunity
Releasing Potential
Achieving Excellence

Phase One

Notes for practitioners and teachers

Phase One falls largely within the Communication, Language and Literacy area of learning in the Early Years Foundation Stage. In particular, it will support linking sounds and letters in the order in which they occur in words, and naming and sounding the letters of the alphabet. It also draws on and promotes other areas of learning described in the Early Years Foundation Stage (EYFS), particularly Personal, Social and Emotional Development and Creative Development, where, for example, music plays a key part in developing children's language. Phase One contributes to the provision for Communication, Language and Literacy; it does not constitute the whole language provision.

The activities in Phase One are mainly adult-led with the intention of teaching young children important basic elements of the Letters and Sounds programme such as oral segmenting and blending of familiar words. However, it is equally important to sustain and draw upon worthwhile, freely chosen activities that are provided for children in good early years settings and Reception classes. The aim is to embed the Phase One adult-led activities in a language-rich provision that serves the best interests of the children by fully recognising their propensity for play and its importance in their development.

It follows that the high quality play activities which typify good provision will offer lots of opportunities to enrich children's language across the six areas of learning:

- Personal, Social and Emotional Development

- Communication, Language and Literacy

- Problem Solving, Reasoning and Numeracy

- Knowledge and Understanding of the World

- Physical Development

- Creative Development.

Practitioners and teachers will need to be alert to the opportunities afforded for language development through children's play, and link learning from the Letters and Sounds programme with all six areas.

Enjoying and sharing books

Experience shows that children benefit hugely by exposure to books from an early age.

Right from the start, lots of opportunities should be provided for children to engage with books that fire their imagination and interest. They should be encouraged to choose and peruse books freely as well as sharing them when read by an adult.

Enjoying and sharing books leads to children seeing them as a source of pleasure and interest and motivates them to value reading.

Planning and progression

Practitioners and teachers should provide daily speaking and listening activities that are well matched to children's developing abilities and interests, drawing upon observations and assessments to plan for progression and to identify children who need additional support, for example to discriminate and produce the sounds of speech.

A rich and varied environment will support children's language learning through Phase One and beyond. Indoor and outdoor spaces should be well planned so that they can be used flexibly. For each aspect in Phase One, there are photographs and captions that illustrate the ways in which the learning environment can be designed to encourage children to explore and apply the knowledge and skills to which they have been introduced through the activities.

Oral blending and segmenting the sounds in words are an integral part of the later stages of Phase One. Whilst recognising alliteration (words that begin with the same sound) is important as children develop their ability to tune into speech sounds, the main objective should be segmenting words into their component sounds, and especially blending the component sounds all through a word.

Exploring the sounds in words should occur as opportunities arise throughout the course of the day's activities, as well as in planned adult-led sessions with groups and individual children. Children's curiosity in letter shapes and written words should be fostered throughout Phase One to help them make a smooth transition to Phase Two, when grapheme–phoneme correspondences are introduced. There is no requirement that children should have mastered all the skills in Phase One (e.g. the ability to supply a rhyming word) before beginning Phase Two.

Modelling listening and speaking

The ways in which practitioners and teachers model speaking and listening, interact and talk with children are critical to the success of Phase One activities and to promoting children's speaking and listening skills more widely. The key adult behaviours can be summarised as follows.

- Listen to encourage talking – time spent listening to children talk to each other, and listening to individuals without too frequent interruption, helps them to use more, and more relevant, language. This provides practitioners with insights into children's learning in order to plan further learning, that is make assessments for learning. Practitioners should recognise that waiting time is constructive. It allows children to think about what has been said, gather their thoughts and frame their replies.

- Model good listening. This includes making eye contact with speakers, asking the sort of questions attentive listeners ask and commenting on what has been said. Effective practitioners adapt their spoken interventions to give children ample opportunities to extend their spoken communication.

- Provide good models of spoken English to help young children enlarge their vocabulary and learn, for example, how to structure comprehensible sentences, speak confidently and clearly, and sustain dialogue. Phase One activities are designed to foster these attributes.

Look, listen and note: making assessments for learning

Effective assessment involves careful observation, analysis and review by practitioners of each child's knowledge, skills and understanding in order to track their progress and make informed decisions about planning for the next steps of learning. This assessment for learning (*Early Years Foundation Stage* paras 2.6–2.10, Ref: 00012-2007PCK-EN) is key to the success of Phase One and for enabling practitioners to make principled, professional judgments about when children should begin a systematic phonics programme. For this reason, examples of what practitioners should focus their observations on are included after each set of the Phase One activities under the subheading 'Look, listen and note'. These examples are designed to help practitioners keep a careful eye on children's progress and will help to identify those who may need further practice and support before moving on, as well as supporting those who are capable of making rapid progress. By observing children, listening to them and noting their achievements, practitioners will be well placed to judge how well children are doing and plan next steps.

At the end of each aspect, the 'Considerations' section provides some indications of what practitioners need to reflect on to develop their practice and to ensure that the needs of all the children are met. For example, these sections suggest how activities may be extended where appropriate to provide greater challenge and encourage children to apply their developing language knowledge and skills more widely.

Seven aspects and three strands

Phase One activities are arranged under the following seven aspects.

- Aspect 1: General sound discrimination – environmental sounds
- Aspect 2: General sound discrimination – instrumental sounds
- Aspect 3: General sound discrimination – body percussion
- Aspect 4: Rhythm and rhyme
- Aspect 5: Alliteration
- Aspect 6: Voice sounds
- Aspect 7: Oral blending and segmenting

While there is considerable overlap between these aspects, the overarching aim is for children to experience regular, planned opportunities to listen carefully and talk extensively about what they hear, see and do. The boundaries between each strand are flexible and not fixed: practitioners should plan to integrate the activities according to the developing abilities and interests of the children in the setting.

Each aspect is divided into three strands.

- Tuning into sounds (auditory discrimination)
- Listening and remembering sounds (auditory memory and sequencing)
- Talking about sounds (developing vocabulary and language comprehension).

Activities within the seven aspects are designed to help children:

1. listen attentively;
2. enlarge their vocabulary;
3. speak confidently to adults and other children;
4. discriminate phonemes;
5. reproduce audibly the phonemes they hear, in order, all through the word;
6. use sound-talk to segment words into phonemes.

The ways in which practitioners and teachers interact and talk with children are critical to developing children's speaking and listening. This needs to be kept in mind throughout all phase one activities.

List of activities

Key

This icon indicates that the activity
can be viewed on the DVD.

Letters and Sounds: **Phase One**

Aspect 1: **Environmental sounds**

Join children in their play to extend their talk and enrich their vocabulary.

Explore with children the sounds different animals make, including imaginary ones such as dragons.

Encourage children to use language for thinking by asking open questions such as What does it feel like to be in the tunnel?

Children enjoy experimenting with the sounds different objects can make.

Making large movements with swirling ribbons helps to develop physical skills necessary for writing.

Using a more unusual role-play area inspires children to use language for a range of purposes.

Aspect 1: General sound discrimination – environmental sounds

Tuning into sounds

Main purpose

■ To develop children's listening skills and awareness of sounds in the environment

Listening walks

This is a listening activity that can take place indoors or outdoors.

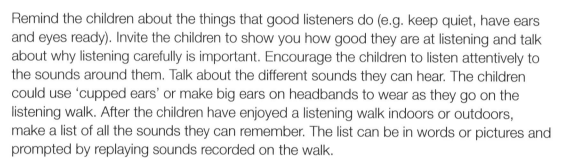

Remind the children about the things that good listeners do (e.g. keep quiet, have ears and eyes ready). Invite the children to show you how good they are at listening and talk about why listening carefully is important. Encourage the children to listen attentively to the sounds around them. Talk about the different sounds they can hear. The children could use 'cupped ears' or make big ears on headbands to wear as they go on the listening walk. After the children have enjoyed a listening walk indoors or outdoors, make a list of all the sounds they can remember. The list can be in words or pictures and prompted by replaying sounds recorded on the walk.

A listening moment

This is another activity that can take place indoors or outdoors.

Remind the children how to be good listeners and invite them to show how good they are at listening by remembering all the sounds they hear when they listen for a moment. It may be useful to use a sand timer to illustrate, for example, the passing of half a minute. Ask them what made each sound and encourage them to try to make the sound themselves.

Drum outdoors

Give each child a beater or make drumsticks, for example from short pieces of dowel. Encourage the children to explore the outdoor area and discover how different sounds are made by tapping or stroking, with their beaters, a wooden door, a wire fence, a metal slide, and a few items such as pipes and upturned pots you have 'planted'.

The activity could be recorded and/or photographed.

Ask each child to demonstrate their favourite sound for the rest of the group. The whole group can join in and copy.

Ask each child to take up position ready to make their favourite sound. An adult or a child acts as conductor and raises a beater high in the air to signal the children to play loudly and lowers it to signal playing softly.

Teddy is lost in the jungle

One child (the rescuer) is taken aside while a teddy bear is hidden somewhere in the room. Tell the other children they are going to guide the rescuer to the teddy by singing louder as the rescuer gets closer to, or quietly as the rescuer moves further away from the teddy. Alternatively lead the children in singing a familiar song, rhyme or jingle, speeding up and slowing down to guide the rescuer.

Sound lotto

There are many commercially produced sound lotto games that involve children matching pictures to a taped sound. This can be an adult-led small group activity or can be provided within the setting as a freely chosen activity.

Look, listen and note

Look, listen and note how well children:

- recall sounds they have heard;

- discriminate between the sounds;

- describe the sounds they hear.

Listening and remembering sounds

Main purpose

- Further development of vocabulary and children's identification and recollection of the difference between sounds

Sound stories

There are many commercially available resources with prerecorded sounds to illustrate a simple sequence of events (e.g. a thunderstorm). Each child selects two or three picture cards that match the sounds, places the cards in the same order in which the sounds are heard and explains the sequence of events.

Mrs Browning has a box

Turn a box on its side with the opening facing away from the children. One by one place between four and six familiar noisy items (e.g. a set of keys, crisp packet, squeaky toy) into the box, pausing to name them and demonstrate the sound each one makes.

Sing to the tune of 'Old MacDonald' but using your own name or one of the children's:

Mrs...has a box ee i ee i o

And in that box she has a...

Stop. Gesture and ask the children to listen.

Handle one of the objects in the box, out of sight, to make a noise. The children take it in turns to guess what is making the sound. Continue the song but imitating the sound using your voice.

With a zzz zzz here and a zzz zzz there...

Allow the children to take a turn at making a noise from inside the box and use their names as you sing.

Describe and find it

Set up a model farmyard. Describe one of the animals but do not tell the children its name. Say, for example: *This animal has horns, four legs and a tail*. Ask them to say which animal it is. Ask them to make the noise the animal might make. When they are familiar with the game let individual children take the part of the adult and describe the animal for the others to name.

This activity can be repeated with other sets of objects such as zoo animals, toy sets based on transport (e.g. aeroplane, car, train, bus, boat) and musical instruments. It can be made more challenging by introducing sets of random objects to describe and name.

Look, listen and note

Look, listen and note how well children:

■ describe what they see;

■ identify the animals and imitate the sounds;

■ add new words to their vocabulary.

> ### Talking about sounds

Main purpose

■ To make up simple sentences and talk in greater detail about sounds

Socks and shakers

Partially fill either opaque plastic bottles or the toes of socks with noisy materials (e.g. rice, peas, pebbles, marbles, shells, coins). Ask the children to shake the bottles or socks and identify what is inside from the sound the items make. From the feel and the sound of the noisy materials encourage the children to talk about them. Ask questions such as: *Where might we find shells and pebbles?*

Favourite sounds

Make a poster or use a whiteboard for the children to record their favourite sounds pictorially. Invite them to put their sounds in order of popularity and talk about the ones they like the best. Ask the children to think about sounds that they do not like (e.g. stormy weather, barking dogs, car horns, crying babies) and to say why.

Enlivening stories

Involve the children in songs and stories, enlivened by role-play, props and repeated sounds, for example acting out:

Humpty Dumpty sat on a wall,

Humpty Dumpty had a great fall (bump, crash, bang!)

All the King's horses and all the King's men (gallop, gallop, gallop)

Couldn't put Humpty together again (boo, hoo, boo, hoo, boo, hoo).

Look, listen and note

Look, listen and note how well children:

- identify different sounds and place them in a context;

- identify similar sounds;

- make up sentences to talk about sounds;

- join in the activities and take turns to participate.

Considerations for practitioners working with Aspect 1

- Use picture or symbol prompts to remind the children how to be a good listener. These could be displayed on the wall, on a soft toy or in a quiet listening den.

- As with all listening and attention activities, it is important to be aware that a busy environment can really hinder a child's ability to tune in. Keep a listening area free from overly distracting wall displays, posters and resources in order to support very young children or those who find it hard to focus on listening.

- A small group size is preferable, to allow all of the children to have sufficient time to participate in and respond to the activity.

- Using gestures such as a finger to the lips alongside 'shhh' and a hand to the ear alongside *listen* will give vital clues to children who have difficulty with understanding or those who find it difficult to listen to the spoken instruction alone.

- Scan the group before giving any sound cue. Use a child's name if necessary then make the sound immediately that you have their attention.

- If parents or carers speak languages other than English, find out the word for 'listen' in the school community languages and use it when appropriate.

- If the children seem to recognise an object, but can't recall its name, help them by prompting with questions, such as: *What would you do with it? Where would you find it?*

- As you lead the singing, take care to slow the song down. Slowing the pace can make a huge difference, helping children to understand the language used as well as giving them time to prepare and join in with the words or sounds.

- Forget conventional sound effects. For example, dogs don't always bark *woof*. Big dogs can sound like *WUW WUW WUW* and little ones give a squeaky *Rap rap*. Vary the voice to add interest. These sounds are often more fun and even easier for the child to attempt to copy. Be daring. Include some less conventional animals (e.g. a parrot, a wolf) and see what sounds you come up with. You might include dinosaurs – many children love them and no one knows what noises they made so children can be as inventive as they like.

- Where parents or carers speak languages other than English, find out how they represent animal noises. Are woof, meow and quack universal? Which examples from other languages are the most like the real sounds?

Letters and Sounds: Phase One

Aspect 2: Instrumental sounds

Observe how well the children listen to each other as they play in the band.

Note which children can make up simple rhythms.

Children use home-made shakers to explore and learn how sounds can be changed.

In their free play, children enjoy revisiting an adult-led activity.

Playing with musical instruments outdoors encourages children to experiment with the sounds they can hear.

Aspect 2: General sound discrimination – instrumental sounds

These activities promote speaking and listening through the use of musical instruments (either purchased or made by the children). They do not replace the rich music provision necessary for creative development in the wider educational programme.

Tuning into sounds

Main purpose

■ To experience and develop awareness of sounds made with instruments and noise makers

New words to old songs

Take a song or rhyme the children know well and invent new words to suit the purpose and the children's interests. Use percussion instruments to accompany the new lyrics.

Which instrument?

This activity uses two identical sets of instruments. Give the children the opportunity to play one set to introduce the sounds each instrument makes and name them all. Then one child hides behind a screen and chooses one instrument from the identical set to play. The other children have to identify which instrument has been played.

Develop the activity by playing a simple rhythm or by adding a song to accompany the instrument (e.g. *There is a music man. Clap your hands*) while the hidden instrument is played. This time the listening children have to concentrate very carefully, discriminating between their own singing and the instrument being played.

Adjust the volume

Two children sit opposite each other with identical instruments. Ask them to copy each other making loud sounds and quiet sounds. It may be necessary to demonstrate with two adults copying each other first. Then try the activity with an adult with one child.

Use cards giving picture or symbol cues to represent loud or quiet (e.g. a megaphone, puppet of a lion; a finger on the lips, puppet of a mouse).[1]

Grandmother's footsteps

'Grandmother' has a range of instruments and the children decide what movement goes with which sound (e.g. shakers for running on tip-toe, triangle for fairy steps).

First an adult will need to model being Grandmother. Then a child takes the role.

---

[1] Activity based on Looking and Listening Pack ©Heywood Middleton & Rochdale Primary Care Trust. Used with kind permission.

Grandmother stands with her back to the others and plays an instrument. The other children move towards Grandmother in the manner of the instrument while it is playing. They stop when it stops. The first person to reach Grandmother takes over that role and the game starts again.

Look, listen and note

Look, listen and note how well children:

- identify and name the instruments being played;

- listen and respond as the instrument is being played.

Listening and remembering sounds

Main purpose

- To listen to and appreciate the difference between sounds made with instruments

Matching sound makers

Show pairs of sound makers (e.g. maracas, triangles) to a small group of children. Place one set of the sound makers in a feely bag.

The children take turns to select a sound maker from the feely bag. Once all the children have selected a sound maker, remind them to listen carefully. Play a matching sound maker. The child with that sound maker stands up and plays it.

This activity can be adapted by playing the sound maker behind a screen so that the children have to identify it by the sound alone[1].

Matching sounds

Invite a small group of children to sit in a circle. Provide a selection of percussion instruments. One child starts the game by playing an instrument. The instrument is then passed round the circle and each child must use it to make the same sound or pattern of sounds as the leader. Start with a single sound to pass round the circle, and then gradually increase the difficulty by having a more complex sequence of sounds or different rhythms.

Look, listen and note

Look, listen and note how well children:

- are able to remember and repeat a rhythm;

- discriminate and reproduce loud and quiet sounds;

- are able to start and stop playing at the signal.

[1] Activity based on Looking and Listening Pack ©Heywood Middleton & Rochdale Primary Care Trust. Used with kind permission.

Main purpose

■ To use a wide vocabulary to talk about the sounds instruments make.

Story sounds

As you read or tell stories, encourage the children to play their instruments in different ways (e.g. *Make this instrument sound like giant's footsteps, … a fairy fluttering, … a cat pouncing, … an elephant stamping*). Invite them to make their own suggestions for different characters (e.g. *How might Jack's feet sound as he tiptoes by the sleeping giant? And what about when he runs fast to escape down the beanstalk?*). As the children become familiar with the pattern of the story, each child could be responsible for a different sound.

Hidden instruments

Hide the instruments around the setting, indoors or outdoors, before the children arrive.

Ask the children to look for the instruments. As each instrument is discovered the finder plays it and the rest of the group run to join the finder. Continue until all the instruments are found to make an orchestra.

Musical show and tell

Invite groups of children to perform short instrumental music for others. The others are asked to say what they liked about the music. (They will need a selection of instruments or sound makers and some rehearsal time.)

Animal sounds

Provide a variety of animal puppets or toys and a range of instruments. Encourage the children to play with the instruments and the animals. Discuss matching sounds to the animals. Give a choice of two instruments to represent a child's chosen animal and ask the children to choose which sound is the better fit: *Which one sounds most like the mouse? What do you think, David?*

Look, listen and note

Look, listen and note how well children:

■ choose appropriate words to describe sounds they hear (e.g. *loud, fierce, rough, squeaky, smooth, bumpy, high, low, wobbly*);

■ match sounds to their sources;

■ use sounds imaginatively to represent a story character;

■ express an opinion about what they have heard.

Considerations for practitioners working with Aspect 2

- If a child is reluctant to attempt to copy actions with an instrument, spend a little time building confidence and interest in copying games. Present the child with a set of instruments. Have an identical set to hand. Allow the child to explore and copy back what the child does. Copying children's actions can build confidence and make them feel their contribution is valued. If the activity results in an enjoyable copying game, the adult can subtly attempt to switch roles by taking up a different instrument and making a new sound for the child to copy.

- It will take a little while for some children to make a link between an animal and a corresponding instrument sound. Where necessary to support this, allow plenty of time for the children to play with the animal puppets or toys and talk about the sounds the animals make.

- Provide a variety of animal puppets or toys and a range of instruments. Sit alongside the children to play the instruments and encourage discussion about choices of instruments appropriate for the sounds the animals make.

- Encourage discussion with the children about why they have chosen the instrument to represent their particular animal.

The activities in Aspect 2 also provide opportunities to explore with the children their experience of music at home. Ask parents or carers whether they have any instruments they can bring in, either to play for the children or for the children to look at.

Letters and Sounds: **Phase One**

Aspect 3: **Body percussion**

Listen to the children as they re-enact familiar stories.

Observe how well the children march, stamp and splash to a beat.

Using the outdoor area as much as possible encourages children to explore different ways of making sounds with their bodies.

Stress simple sound patterns to accompany children's mark-making.

Talk with children as they paint and comment on the movements and shapes they are making.

Aspect 3: General sound discrimination – body percussion

Main purpose

■ To develop awareness of sounds and rhythms

Action songs

Singing songs and action rhymes is a vital part of Phase One activities and should be an everyday event. Children need to develop a wide repertoire of songs and rhymes. Be sure to include multi-sensory experiences such as action songs in which the children have to add claps, knee pats and foot stamps or move in a particular way. Add body percussion sounds to nursery rhymes, performing the sounds in time to the beat. Change the body sound with each musical phrase or sentence. Encourage the children to be attentive and to know when to add sounds, when to move, and when to be still.

Listen to the music

Introduce one musical instrument and allow each child in the small group to try playing it. Ask the children to perform an action when the instrument is played (e.g. clap, jump, wave). The children can take turns at being leader. Ask the child who is leading to produce different movements for others to copy. As the children become more confident, initiate simple repeated sequences of movement (e.g. clap, clap, jump). Suggest to the children that they could make up simple patterns of sounds for others to copy. Ask the children to think about how the music makes them feel and let them move to the music.[1]

Roly poly

Rehearse the rhyme with the actions (rotating hand over hand as in the song 'Wind the bobbin up').

Ro … ly … po … ly … ever … so … slowly

Ro … ly … poly faster.

(Increase the speed of the action as you increase the speed of the rhyme.)

Now add in new verses, such as:

Stamp … your … feet … ever … so … slowly

Stamp … your feet faster.

Ask the children to suggest sounds and movements to be incorporated into the song.

Say hello ever so quietly

Say HELLO LOUDER!

[1] Activity based on Looking and Listening Pack ©Heywood Middleton & Rochdale Primary Care Trust. Used with kind permission.

00281-2007BKT-EN

Look, listen and note

Look, listen and note how well children:

- produce contrasts in rhythm, speed and loudness;

- join in with words and actions to familiar songs;

- articulate words clearly;

- keep in time with the beat;

- copy the sounds and actions;

- make up patterns of sounds.

Listening and remembering sounds

Main purpose

- To distinguish between sounds and to remember patterns of sound

Follow the sound

Invite a small group of children to sit in a circle. The adult begins by producing a body percussion sound which is then 'passed' to the child sitting next to them such as clap, clap, clap. The sound is to be passed around the circle until it returns to the adult. Ask: *Do you think that the sound stayed the same all the way round? What changed? Did it get faster or slower?* Make the activity more difficult by introducing a simple sequence of sounds for the children to pass on (e.g. clap, stamp, clap).

Noisy neighbour 1

This game needs two adults to lead it.

Tell a simple story about a noisy neighbour and invite the children to join in. Begin with: *Early one morning, the children were all fast sleep –* (ask the children to close their eyes and pretend to sleep) – *when all of a sudden they heard a sound from the house next door.*

At this point the second adult makes a sound from behind the screen.

The story teller continues: *Wake up children. What's that noise?*

The children take it in turns to identify the sound and then the whole group are encouraged to join in with: *Noisy neighbour, please be quiet. We are trying to sleep.*

Repeat the simple story line with another sound (e.g. snoring, brushing teeth, munching cornflakes, yawning, stamping feet, washing).

Encourage the children to add their own ideas to the story about the noisy neighbour.

Look, listen and note

Look, listen and note how well children:

- copy a body percussion sound or pattern of sounds;

- identify hidden sounds;

- suggest ideas and create new sounds for the story.

Talking about sounds

Main purpose

- To talk about sounds we make with our bodies and what the sounds mean

Noisy neighbour 2

(See 'Noisy neighbour 1' above.)

Ask the children to suggest a suitable ending to the story. Discuss noises they like, noises that make them excited and noises that make them feel cross or sad. Ask when it is a good time to be noisy, and when it is best to be quiet or speak softly (e.g. when we need to listen). List the suggestions.

Ask *Is this a time to be noisy or quiet?* as you present scenarios such as when children are:

- at the swimming pool;

- in the library;

- at a party;

- with someone who is asleep;

- in the park;

- at a friend's house when the friend is poorly;

- playing hide and seek.

Words about sounds

It is important that adults engage with children in their freely chosen activities and introduce vocabulary that helps them to discriminate and contrast sounds, for example:

- *slow*, *fast*;

- *quiet*, *loud*;

- *long*, *short*;

- type of sound (*click*, *stamp*, etc.);

- type of movement (*rock*, *march*, *skip*, etc.).

Start with simple opposites that are obviously different (e.g. *loud*, *quiet*).

Listen to what the children have to say about the sounds they hear and then build on and expand their contributions and ideas.

The Pied Piper

Tell the story of the Pied Piper of Hamelin. Use different instruments for the Piper to play, with children moving in different ways in response. The child at the front decides on the movement and the rest of the group move in the same way. They follow the leader around the indoor or outdoor space, marching, skipping and hopping – vary the pace and describe the action: *Fast, faster, slow, slower*.

Introduce and model new words by acting them out (e.g. *briskly, rapidly, lazily, sluggishly, energetically*) for the children to copy and explore by acting them out in different ways.

Look, listen and note

Look, listen and note how well children:

- use language to make different endings to the story;

- use a wide vocabulary to talk about the sounds they hear;

- group sounds according to different criteria (e.g. *loud, quiet, slow, fast*).

Considerations for practitioners working with Aspect 3

- Remind the children to **look** and **listen** to the adult and also to each other.

- It might be necessary to demonstrate the sounds to the children before each activity starts in order to 'tune them in' and to encourage them to describe the sounds they hear.

- Be aware that some children may have difficulty coordinating the movements or actions to accompany songs and games. Give children plenty of time and space to practise large-scale movements every day.

- Some children may find it difficult to monitor their own volume without adult support.

Letters and Sounds: **Phase One**

Aspect 4: **Rhythm and rhyme**

Children enjoy listening to rhymes and inventing their own.

Enjoying and sharing books leads to children seeing them as a source of pleasure and interest.

Children need to build a stock of rhymes through hearing them repeated over and over again.

Encourage children's word play by inventing new rhymes with them such as *Hickory, Dickory Dable, the mouse ran up the .....*

Remind children of rhymes they know when you join them in the role play area *Miss Polly had a dolly ...!*

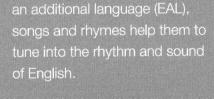

For children learning English as an additional language (EAL), songs and rhymes help them to tune into the rhythm and sound of English.

Aspect 4: Rhythm and rhyme

Main purpose

■ To experience and appreciate rhythm and rhyme and to develop awareness of rhythm and rhyme in speech

Rhyming books

Regularly include rhyming books as part of the daily book-sharing session. Read these books with plenty of intonation and expression so that the children tune into the rhythm of the language and the rhyming words. Encourage the children to join in with repetitive phrases such as *Run, run, as fast as you can, You can't catch me, I'm the Gingerbread Man.* Wherever possible make the activity multi-sensory to intensify learning and enjoyment.

Learning songs and rhymes

Make sure that singing and rhyming activities are part of the daily routine in small-group time and that extracts are repeated incidentally as events occur (e.g. *It's raining, it's pouring* as the children get ready to go outdoors in wet weather). Play with rhyming words throughout the course of the day and have fun with them. Sing or chant nursery rhymes and encourage the children to move in an appropriate way (e.g. rock gently to the beat of 'See Saw Marjorie Daw', march to the beat of 'Tom, Tom the Piper's Son' and 'The Grand Old Duke of York', skip to the beat of 'Here We Go Round the Mulberry Bush').

Listen to the beat

Use a variety of percussion instruments to play different rhythms. Remind the children to use their listening ears and to move in time to the beat – fast, slow, skipping, marching, etc. Keep the beat simple at first (e.g. suitable for marching) then move on to more complex rhythms for the children to skip or gallop to.

Our favourite rhymes

Support a group of children to compile a book of their favourite rhymes and songs. They could represent the rhymes in any way they choose. The book can be used to make choices about which rhyme to say during singing time, or used for making independent choices in the book corner. Children may choose to act as teacher selecting rhymes for others to perform, individually or as a group.

Have a bag of objects which represent rhymes (e.g. a toy spider to represent 'Incy Wincy Spider', a toy bus for 'The Wheels on the Bus') and invite the children to choose their favourite.

Rhyming soup

Ask a small group to sit in a circle so they can see a selection of rhyming objects (e.g. rat, hat, cat) placed on the floor. Use a bowl and spoon as props to act out the song. Invite the children, in turn, to choose an object to put into the soup and place it in the bowl. After each turn, stir the soup and sing the following song to recite the growing list of things that end up in the soup.

Sing the first part of the song to the tune of 'Pop Goes the Weasel':

I'm making lots of silly soup

I'm making soup that's silly

I'm going to cook it in the fridge

To make it nice and chilly

In goes... a fox... a box... some socks...

Rhyming bingo

Give each child in a small group a set of three pictures of objects with rhyming names. (Such pictures are readily available commercially.) Hide in a bag a set of pictures or objects matching the pictures you have given to the children.

The children take turns to draw out of the bag one object or picture at a time. Invite the children to call out when they see an object or picture that rhymes with theirs and to collect it from the child who has drawn it from the bag.

After each rhyming set is completed chant together and list the rhyming names. As you name objects give emphasis to the rhyming pattern.

Playing with words

Gather together a set of familiar objects with names that have varying syllable patterns (e.g. pencil, umbrella, camera, xylophone). Show the objects to the children, name them and talk about what they are used for. Wait for the children to share some of their experiences of the objects; for instance, some of them will have used a camera. Then encourage them to think about how the name of the object sounds and feels as they say it. Think about the syllables and clap them out as you say each word. Then clap the syllables for a word without saying it and ask: *What object could that be?*

As children gain confidence try some long words like *binoculars, telephone, dinosaur.*

Look, listen and note

Look, listen and note how well children:

- understand the pattern of syllables in the words presented to them;

- sing or chant the rhyming string along with the adult;

- recognise that the words rhyme;

- join in with simple or complex rhythms;

- copy the rhythm;

- keep to the beat.

Listening and remembering sounds

Main purpose

- To increase awareness of words that rhyme and to develop knowledge about rhyme

Rhyming pairs

In a pairs game, use pictures of objects with names that rhyme. The children take it in turns to turn two cards over and keep them if the pictures are a rhyming pair. If they are not a rhyming pair, the cards are turned face down again and the other person has a turn. Start with a small core set of words that can then be extended.

The children need to be familiar with the rhyming word families before they can use them in a game – spend time looking at the pictures and talking about the pairs.

Songs and rhymes

Include a selection of songs within the daily singing session which involve children in experimenting with their voices. Simple nursery rhymes, such as 'Hickory, Dickory, Dock' provide an opportunity for children to join in with *wheeee* as the mouse falls down. Use this to find related words that rhyme: *dock*, *clock*, *tick-tock*. Substitute alternative rhyming sounds to maintain children's interest and enjoyment.

Finish the rhyme

Use books with predictable rhymes that children are familiar with and then stop as you come to the final word in the rhyme. Invite children to complete it. Use plenty of intonation and expression as the story or rhyme is recounted.

Look, listen and note

Look, listen and note how well children:

- recognise rhyming words;

- listen and attend to the rhyming strings.

Main purpose
- To talk about words that rhyme and to produce rhyming words

Rhyming puppets

Make up silly rhyming names for a pair of puppets (e.g. *Fizzy Wizzy Lizzy* and *Hob Tob Bob*). Introduce the puppets to a small group and invite them to join in story telling, leaving gaps for the children to fill in rhyming words, for example:

Are you poorly Lizzy? Oh dear.
Fizzy Wizzy Lizzy is feeling sick and…dizzy.

Bob is very excited. Today he is going to be a builder.
Hob Tob Bob has got a new…job.

Odd one out

Put out three objects or pictures, two with names that rhyme and one with a name that does not. Ask the child to identify the 'odd one out': the name that does not rhyme. Start with a small set of words that can then be extended. The children need to be familiar with the rhyming word families before they can use them in a game – spend time looking at the pictures and talking about the pairs.

I know a word

Throughout the course of daily activities, encourage the children to think about and play with rhyming words. The adult begins with the prompt *I know a word that rhymes with cat, you need to put one on your head and the word is…hat.* This can be used for all sorts of situations and also with some children's names: *I know a girl who is holding a dolly, she is in the book corner and her name is…Molly.* As children become familiar with rhyme, they will supply the missing word themselves.

Look, listen and note
Look, listen and note how well children:

- generate their own rhymes;

- complete sentences using appropriate rhyming words;

- make a series of words that rhyme.

Considerations for practitioners working with Aspect 4

- It is important for children to experience a rich repertoire of poems, rhymes and songs. They need to build a stock of rhymes through hearing them repeated in different contexts. Parents and carers can play a valuable role in developing children's repertoires of rhymes. Keep parents and carers informed of any new rhymes you are learning with the children so that the adults can join in when the children start to sing them at home.

- For children learning EAL, songs and rhymes are a particularly effective way to remember whole sentences and phrases by tuning into the rhythm that accompanies them. This in itself is good practice for developing the speech patterns of the language; it is also important to attach meaning and ensure that contexts are understood.

- Encouraging nonsense rhymes is a good way for children to begin to generate and produce rhyme. While a child is developing speech sounds the normal immaturities in their speech may mean their version of a word is different from that of the adults in the setting (e.g. the adult prompts with *You shall have a fish on a little…*and the child joins in with *dit*). The adult then repeats back the correct articulation, '*dish*'.

- When children experiment with nonsense rhymes they are not confined by their own learned versions of words and so can tune into and produce rhyming patterns.

- Keep the songs slow so you can emphasise the rhyming patterns.

- Collecting a set of objects or producing pictures of objects with rhyming names can be time-consuming but this resource is essential to build experience of rhyme into children's play. A set of cards from a commercially available rhyming lotto set can prove to be a versatile resource for many different activities.

- Generating rhymes is a difficult skill to master. Accept all the children's suggestions. Where the children do manage to fill in with the target rhyming word, congratulate them on having done so and draw attention to the rhyming pattern.

- Children learning EAL often internalise chunks of language and may not hear where one word starts and another ends. They may continue to use many of these chunks of language for some time before they begin to segment the speech stream in order to use the constituent words in new contexts.

- When children can supply a list of rhyming words and non-words, after being given a start, they can be considered to be well on the way to grasping rhyme (e.g. adult says *cat, mat, sat…*and the child continues *fat, pat, mat, rat*). However, children may well be at a later phase of this programme before they can do this. **There is no need to delay starting Phase Two until children have mastered rhyming.**

Letters and Sounds: **Phase One**

Aspect 5: **Alliteration**

After children have enjoyed their singing games, make the resources freely available to them to explore for themselves and to act out 'being the teacher'.

Make sure the book collection includes books with lots of alliterative rhymes and jingles.

Play alongside children in a café and place an order: *'Please may I have some juicy jelly'* or *'sizzling sausages'* or *'chunky chips'*.

Join children at the water tray and introduce alliterative tongue twisters such as *She sells seashells*.

Aspect 5: Alliteration

Main purpose

■ To develop understanding of alliteration

I spy names

With a small group of children sitting in a circle, start the game by saying *I spy someone whose name begins with…* and give the sound of the first letter, for example 's' for Satish. Then ask: *Who can it be?* Satish stands up, everyone says his name and he carries on the game, saying *I spy someone whose name begins with…*, and so on. If any children call out the name before the child with that name, still let the child whose name it is take the next turn.

If the children find separating out the first sound too hard in the early stages, the adult can continue to be the caller until they get the hang of it.

Sounds around

Make sure that word play with initial sounds is commonplace. Include lots of simple tongue twisters to ensure that children enjoy experimenting with words that are alliterative. Use opportunities as they occur incidentally to make up tongue twisters by using children's names, or objects that are of particular personal interest to them (e.g. *David's dangerous dinosaur, Millie's marvellous, magic mittens*).

Making aliens

Before the activity begins, think of some strange names for alien creatures. The alien names must be strings of non-words with the same initial sound, for example:

Ping pang poo pop,
Mig mog mully mo,
Fo fi fandle fee.

Write them down as a reminder.

Talk to the children about the names and help them to imagine what the strange creatures might look like. Provide creative or construction materials for the children to make their own alien.

Comment as the children go about shaping the aliens and use the aliens' strange names. Invite the children to display their aliens along with the aliens' names.

Make the pattern clearer by emphasising the initial sound of an alien's name. Draw the children's attention to the way you start each word with the shape of your lips, teeth and tongue.

Digging for treasure

Collect two sets of objects suitable for use in the sand tray. Each set of objects must have names beginning with the same initial sound. Choose initial sounds for each set that sound very different from one another. Bury the objects in preparation for the session. As the children uncover the treasure, group the objects by initial sound and each time another is added recite the content of that set: *Wow! You've found a car. Now we have a cup, a cow, a candle and a car.*

Bertha goes to the zoo

Set up a small toy zoo and join the children as they play with it. Use a toy bus and a bag of animal toys with names starting with the same sound (e.g. a lion, a lizard, a leopard, a llama and a lobster) to act out this story. Chant the following rhyme and allow each child in turn to draw an animal out of the bag and add an animal name to the list of animals spotted at the zoo.

Bertha the bus is going to the zoo,
Who does she see as she passes through?
… a pig, a panda, a parrot and a polar bear.

Look, listen and note

Look, listen and note how well children:

- identify initial sounds of words;

- reproduce the initial sounds clearly and recognisably;

- make up their own alliterative phrases.

Listening and remembering sounds

Main purpose

- To listen to sounds at the beginning of words and hear the differences between them

Tony the Train's busy day

Use a toy train and selection of objects starting with the same sound. A small group of children sits in a circle or facing the front so they can see objects placed on the floor. Use the props to act out a story with the train.

It was going to be a busy day for Tony. He had lots to do before bedtime. So many packages to deliver and so many passengers to carry. He set out very early, leaving all the other engines at the station, and hurried off down the track, clackedy clack down the track, clackedy clack down the track…

But he hadn't gone very far when…!!! He saw something up ahead lying on the tracks. 'Oh no!' yelled Tony. 'I must s – t – o – p.' And he did stop, just in time. To Tony's surprise there on the track lay a big brown bear, fast asleep.

'I had better warn the others,' thought Tony and so he hurried back to the station, clackedy clack going back, clackedy clack going back. Tony arrived at the station quite out of puff. 'Whatever is the matter?' said the other engines. 'Toot, toot, mind the…big, brown bear' panted Thomas. 'He's fast asleep on the track.' 'Thank you,' said the others, 'We certainly will.'

Continue with the whole object set and encourage the children to join in with saying the growing list of objects. Remember to give emphasis to the initial sound.

The aim is to have the group chant along with you as you recite the growing list of objects that Tony finds lying on the track. Make up your own story using the props and ask: *What do you think happens next?*

Musical corners

Put a chair in each corner of the room, or outdoors. Collect four sets of objects, each set containing objects with names that start with the same sound. (Four different initial sounds are represented.) Keep back one object from each set and place the remaining sets on each of the four chairs.

At first, the children sit in a circle or facing you. Name each of the four sets of objects, giving emphasis to the initial sound.

Explain that now there will be music to move around or dance to and that when the music stops the children are to listen. You will show them an object and they should go to the corner where they think it belongs.

Our sound box/bag

Make collections of objects with names beginning with the same sound. Create a song, such as 'What have we got in our sound box today?' and then show the objects one at a time. Emphasise the initial sound (e.g. s-s-s-snake, s-s-s-sock, s-s-s-sausage)

Look, listen and note

Look, listen and note how well children:

■ can recall the list of objects beginning with the same sound;

■ can offer their own sets of objects and ideas to end the story;

■ discriminate between the sounds and match to the objects correctly.

Main purpose

■ To explore how different sounds are articulated, and to extend understanding of alliteration

Name play

Call out a child's name and make up a fun sentence starting with the name (e.g. *Ben has a big, bouncy ball, Kulvinder keeps kippers in the kitchen, Tim has ten, tickly toes, Fiona found a fine, fat frog*). Ask the children to think up similar sentences for their own names to share with others.

Mirror play

Provide a mirror for each child or one large enough for the group to gather in front of. Play at making faces and copying movements of the lips and tongue. Introduce sound making in the mirror and discuss the way lips move, for example, when sounding out 'p' and 'b', the way that tongues poke out for 'th', the way teeth and lips touch for 'f' and the way lips shape the sounds 'sh' and 'm'.

Silly soup

Provide the children with a selection of items with names that begin with the same sound. Show them how you can make some 'silly soup' by putting 'ingredients' (e.g. a banana, bumble bee and bug) into a pan in the role-play area.

Allow the children to play and concoct their own recipes. Play alongside them without influencing their choices. Commentate and congratulate the children on their silly recipes. Recite each child's list of chosen ingredients. Make the pattern clear by emphasising the initial sound. By observing mouth movements draw the children's attention to the way we start each word and form sounds.

Look, listen and note

Look, listen and note how well children:

■ can articulate speech sounds clearly;

■ select an extended range of words that start with the same sound.

Considerations for practitioners working with Aspect 5

- Singing rhymes and songs with alliterative lines such as 'Sing a Song of Sixpence' and playing with jingles such as 'Can you count the candles on the cake?' helps to tune children's ears to the relationships between the sound structures of words. Ultimately children need to be able to isolate the initial phoneme from the rest of word (e.g. to be able to say that 'nose' begins with the sound 'n'). Children need to have a wealth of experience of hearing words that begin with the same sound so it is important to keep practising familiar tongue twisters and also to be inventive with new ones to model alliterative possibilities to the children.

- Do not expect all the children to be able to produce a full range of initial sounds or be able to produce the initial clusters such as 'sp' for spoon. Just make sure that each child's attention is gained before reciting the string of sounds so that they can experience the initial sound pattern as it is modelled for them.

- These activities may reveal speech difficulties that may require investigation by a specialist such as the local speech and language therapist.

- Not all children will be happy to participate in copying games. Some may feel self-conscious or be anxious about getting the game wrong. One way to encourage copying is to lead the way by copying what the children do in the mirror and encouraging them to copy one another before asking them to copy your sounds and movements.

- Take care to whisper when modelling quiet sounds. Do not add an 'uh' to the end of sounds:
  - 'ssss' not 'suh'
  - 'mmm' not 'muh'
  - 't' not 'tuh'
  - 'sh' not 'shuh'.

- Some children may be aware of the letter shapes that represent some sounds. While grapheme–phoneme correspondences are not introduced until Phase Two, it is important to be observant of those children who can identify letter shapes and sounds and to encourage their curiosity and interest.

- Be prepared to accept suggestions from children learning EAL who have a well-developed vocabulary in their home language, but be aware that words in home languages will not always conveniently start with the same sound as the English translation. Children very soon distinguish between vocabulary in their home language and English.

Letters and Sounds: **Phase One**

Aspect 6: **Voice sounds**

Encourage children to replicate water noises with sounds such as *drip, bubble bubble, swoosh*.

As children explore the texture of shaving foam, pasta shapes or foamy water, introduce words that may be new to them such as *smooth frothy crunchy*.

As you watch children on the climbing frame, encourage them to vocalise *'Weeee!'*.

When children act out familiar stories, encourage them to use sound effects like *swish swish through the grass, squelch squelch in the mud, splishy sploshy through the rain*.

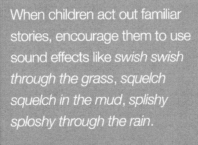

Aspect 6: Voice sounds

Main purpose

■ To distinguish between the differences in vocal sounds, including oral blending and segmenting

Mouth movements

Explore different mouth movements with children – blowing, sucking, tongue stretching and wiggling. Practising these movements regularly to music can be fun and helps children with their articulation.

Voice sounds

Show children how they can make sounds with their voices, for example:

■ *Make your voice go down a slide – wheee!*

■ *Make your voice bounce like a ball – boing, boing*

■ *Sound really disappointed – oh*

■ *Hiss like a snake – ssssss*

■ *Keep everyone quiet – shshshsh*

■ *Gently moo like a cow – mmmoooo*

■ *Look astonished – oooooo!*

■ *Be a steam train – chchchchch*

■ *Buzz like a bumble bee – zzzzzzz*

■ *Be a clock – tick tock.*

This can be extended by joining single speech sounds into pairs (e.g. *ee-aw* like a donkey).

Making trumpets

Make amplifiers (trumpet shapes) from simple cones of paper or lightweight card and experiment by making different noises through the cones. Model sounds for the children: the up and down wail of a siren, the honk of a fog horn, a *peep, peep, peep* of a bird. Contrast loud and soft sounds. Invite the children to share their favourite sound for the rest of the group to copy. Use the trumpets to sound out phonemes that begin each child's name.

Metal Mike

Encourage a small group of children to sit in a circle or facing the front so they can see you and Metal Mike (a toy robot computer). Have ready a bag of pictures of objects (e.g. cat, dog, mug, sock) and sound out and blend the phonemes in their names. Ask each child in turn to take out a picture or an object from a bag. Hold it up and tell the group that Metal Mike is a computer and so he talks with a robot voice. Ask the children to name the object as Metal Mike would and demonstrate it for them in a robotic voice (e.g. 'c-a-t'). Feed the object or picture into Metal Mike and encourage the group first to listen to you and then join in as you say the word exaggerating the sound of each phoneme, followed by blending the phonemes to make the word.

Look, listen and note

Look, listen and note how well children:

■ distinguish between the differences in vocal sounds.

Listening and remembering sounds

Main purpose

■ To explore speech sounds

Chain games

Working with a small group of children, an adult makes a long sound with their voice, varying the pitch (e.g. *eeeeeee*). The next person repeats the sound and continues as the next joins in, to form a chain. The sound gets passed as far round the circle as possible. Start again when the chain is broken.

Target sounds

Give each child a target sound to put into a story when they hear a particular word or character (e.g. make a 'ch' sound when they hear the word 'train').

Start with a single sound that the small group of children can make together when they hear a target word. Be prepared to prompt initially and leave pauses in your reading to make it obvious where the sounds are required.

Whose voice?

Record some children talking while they are busy with a freely chosen activity and play the recording to a larger group. Can the children identify each other's voices? Create a 'talking book' for the group or class with photographs of each child and help them to record their own voice message – *My name is…, I like singing*, etc.

Sound lotto 2

Record the children using their voices to make suitable sounds for simple pictures (e.g. of animals, a steam train, a doorbell, a clock). Ask them to listen to the recording later and match each sound to a picture.

Look, listen and note

Look, listen and note how well children:

■ sustain their listening throughout a story;

■ listen for a target word or character and respond with an appropriate associated speech sound;

■ remember the sound sequence and produce it when required;

■ recognise their own and each other's voices, including a recorded voice.

Talking about sounds

Main purpose

■ To talk about the different sounds that we can make with our voices

Give me a sound

After making a sound with your voice, talk about the 'features' of the sound with the children – was it a long sound, a loud sound, did it change from high to low, etc.? Introduce vocabulary gradually with examples and visual cues (e.g. symbols and pictures) to help the children who have difficulty understanding. Then introduce new vocabulary to the children to help them describe the sound (e.g. to talk about high and low pitch).

Sound story time

Discuss with the children how they can use their voices to add sounds to stories such as *Bear Hunt*, *Chicken Licken* or *The Three Billy Goats Gruff*.

Repeat favourite rhymes and poems in different voices together (e.g. whispering, growling, shouting, squeaking) and discuss the differences.

Watch my sounds

Provide small mirrors for the children to observe their faces, lips, teeth and tongue as they make different speech sounds and experiment with their voices.

Provide home-made megaphones in the outside area so the children can experiment with different speech sounds and their volume.

Animal noises

Provide simple animal masks, and tails if possible, to encourage the children to dramatise animal movements and sounds.

Singing songs

Provide a wide selection of rhymes and songs on CD or tape so that the children can choose to listen to and join in with their favourites, and can extend their repertoire.

Look, listen and note

Look, listen and note how well children:

■ use appropriate vocabulary to talk about different voice and speech sounds.

Considerations for practitioners working with Aspect 6

■ Changes in voice and exaggerated facial expressions help to support listening and attention by building interest and anticipation. For some children, these clues are also vital to supporting their understanding of the story.

■ Tuning in to what the child is doing and joining in with them tells the child you are listening to them.

■ Children in the early stages of learning EAL may need time to observe others and rehearse the spoken challenge; as in any turn-taking activities they should not be asked to take the first turn.

■ For extension, linguistic diversity and fun, where parents and carers speak languages other than English, find out how they represent, for example, animal noises. Are *woof*, *meow* and *quack* universal? Which examples from other languages are the most like the real sounds?

Letters and Sounds: **Phase One**

Aspect 7: **Oral blending and segmenting**

When children choose to play with the sound talk toys, listen out to how well they are trying to segment words into phonemes.

As children play with the balls, bounce a ball alongside them making the sound 'b' 'b' 'b'

Encourage the children to vocalise as they play on the hoppers 'h' 'h' 'h' 'h'

When children are in the writing area, note whether they are beginning to say their messages aloud as they write, as they have seen adults do.

Aspect 7: Oral blending and segmenting

Main purpose

■ To develop oral blending and segmenting of sounds in words

Oral blending

It is important that the children have plenty of experience of listening to adults modelling oral blending before they are introduced to grapheme–phoneme correspondences. For example, when giving children instructions or asking questions the adult can segment the last word into separate phonemes and then immediately blend the sounds together to say the word (e.g. *It's time to get your c-oa-t, coat!* or *Touch your t-oe-s, toes! Who can touch their f-ee-t, feet?*) Use only single-syllable words for oral blending.

Oral blending can also be modelled from time to time when books are being shared, particularly rhyming books where the last word in a rhyming couplet could be segmented into separate sounds and then blended by the adult.

Toy talk

Introduce to the children a soft toy that can only speak in 'sound-talk'. The children see the toy whispering in the adult's ear. To add to the activity, as the toy whispers the adult repeats the sounds, looks puzzled and then says the word straight afterwards. For example: *What would Charlie like for tea today?* The toy speaks silently in the adult's ear and the adult repeats 'ch-ee-se' looking puzzled and then, says with relief 'cheese!' Now invite the children to see if they can speak like the toy: *Do you think you could try to toy talk? Say ch-ee-se:* (the children repeat 'ch-ee-se'). Ask the toy again *What else would you like?* Be careful to think of items with names of only single syllables (e.g. fish, cake, pie, soup).

Use different scenarios: *What does the toy like to do in the playground?* (hop, skip, jump, run, etc.). As the children become more confident, make some errors – blend 'skim' for 'skip', for example, and ask them to catch you out by giving the correct blend.

Encourage the children to ask the toy questions with yes/no answers (e.g. *Can you sing?* Y-e-s/N-o). Or ask the toy the colour of his bike, his bedroom walls, his jumper, etc. and the toy will answer r-e-d, b-l-ue, g-r-ee-n, m-au-ve.

Clapping sounds

Think of words using the letters 's, a, t, p, i, n' (e.g. *sat, pin, nip, pat, tap, pit, pip*) and sound them out, clapping each phoneme with the children in unison, then blend the phonemes to make the whole word orally.

As children's confidence develops, ask individuals to demonstrate this activity to others.

Which one?

Lay out a selection of familiar objects with names that contain three phonemes (e.g. leaf, sheep, soap, fish, sock, bus). Check that all the children can recognise each object. Bring out the sound-talking toy and ask the children to listen carefully while it says the names of one of the objects in sound-talk so they can help it to put the sounds together and say the word. The toy then sound-talks the word, leaving a short gap between each sound. Encourage the children to say the word and identify the object. All the children can then repeat the sounds and blend them together – it is important that they do this and don't simply listen to the adult doing so.

Cross the river

Choose a selection of objects with two or three phonemes as above. There can be more than one of the same object. Make a river across the floor or ground outside with chalk or ropes. Give each child or pair of children an object and check that all the children know the names of the objects. The toy calls out the name of an object in sound-talk (e.g. p-e-g). The children who have that object blend the sounds to make the word and cross the river.

I spy

Place on the floor or on a table a selection of objects with names containing two or three phonemes (e.g. zip, hat, comb, cup, chain, boat, tap, ball). Check that all the children know the names of the objects. The toy says *I spy with my little eye a z-i-p*. Then invite a child to say the name of the object and hold it up. All the children can then say the individual phonemes and blend them together 'z-i-p, zip'. When the children have become familiar with this game use objects with names that start with the same initial phoneme (e.g. cat, cap, cup, cot, comb, kite). This will really encourage the children to listen and then blend right through the word, rather than relying on the initial sound.

Look, listen and note

Look, listen and note how well children:

- blend phonemes and recognise the whole word;

- say the word and identify the object;

- blend words that begin with the same initial phoneme.

Listening and remembering sounds

Main purpose

- To listen to phonemes within words and to remember them in the order in which they occur

Segmenting

Invite a small group of children to come and talk to the toy in sound-talk, for example just before dinner time: *Let's tell the toy what we eat our dinner with*. Discuss with the children and agree that we use a knife and fork. Then tell the toy in sound-talk which the children repeat. Continue with: *Let's tell the toy what we drink out of*. Confer and agree on 'cup'. Repeat in sound-talk for the toy to listen and then invite the children to do the same.

Ask the children to think of other scenarios which they could tell the toy or let them give him instructions. Then model the sound-talk for the children to repeat. This is teaching the children to segment words into their separate sounds or phonemes and is the reverse of blending. The children will soon begin to start the segmenting themselves.

Leave the sound-talk toy freely available to the children for them to practise and experiment with sound-talk. On special occasions, weekends or holidays, the toy may go on adventures or go to stay at the children's homes. When he returns he will have lots to tell the children about his escapades – in sound-talk.

Say the sounds

When the children are used to hearing the toy say words in sound-talk and blending the individual sounds to make words, you may be able to ask some children to see whether they can speak in sound-talk. Choose some objects with three-phoneme names that you are sure the children know and hide them in a box or bag. Allow one of the children to see an object, and then ask them to try to say the separate sounds in the name of the object, just like the toy does (e.g. *d-u-ck*). The other children then blend the sounds together to make the word. The child can then reveal the object to show whether the other children are right.

Look, listen and note

Look, listen and note how well children:

- segment words into phonemes.

Talking about sounds

Main purpose

- To talk about the different phonemes that make up words

When children are used to oral blending, and can readily blend two and three phonemes to make words, introduce the idea of counting how many phonemes they can hear. For example: *p-i-g*, *pig. If we say the phonemes in that word one by one, how many phonemes can we hear? Let's use our fingers to help us: p-i-g, one, two, three phonemes.*

Look, listen and note

Look, listen and note how well children:

- identify the number of phonemes that make up a given word.

Considerations for practitioners working with Aspect 7

- During Phase One, there is no expectation that children are introduced to letters (graphemes). Of course some children may bring knowledge of letters from home, and be interested in letters they see around them on signs, displays and in books. Practitioners and teachers should certainly respond to children's comments and queries about letters and words in print.

- Children who can hear phonemes in words and sound them out accurately are generally well placed to make a good start in reading and writing.

- Children learning EAL generally learn to hear sounds in words very easily.

- Children need to hear the sounds in the word spoken in sound-talk immediately followed by the whole word. Avoid being tempted to ask any questions in between such as *I wonder what that word can be?* or *Do you know what that word is?* The purpose is to model oral blending and immediately give the whole word.

- It is important only to segment and blend the last word in a sentence or phrase and not words that occur at the beginning or middle of the sentence. Over time and with lots of repetition, the children will get to know the routine and as they gain confidence they will provide the blended word before the adult.

- Using a toy is preferable to a puppet because it is important that children watch the adult's face and mouth to see the sounds being articulated clearly, rather than focusing on the imitated movements of the puppet.

- It is very important to enunciate the phonemes very clearly and not to add an 'uh' to some (e.g. 'sssssss' and not 'suh', 'mmmmmmmm' and not 'muh'). Examples of correct enunciation can be found on the accompanying DVD.

- Avoid using words with adjacent consonants (e.g. 'sp' as in 'spoon') as these will probably be too difficult for children at the early stages of practising blending and segmenting.

- Once children have been introduced to blending and segmenting they should be practised hand in hand as they are reversible processes.

Letters and Sounds: **Phase Two**

Phase Two

(up to 6 weeks)

Contents

Key

This icon indicates that the activity can be viewed on the DVD.

Summary

Children entering Phase Two will have experienced a wealth of listening activities, including songs, stories and rhymes. They will be able to distinguish between speech sounds and many will be able to blend and segment words orally. Some will also be able to recognise spoken words that rhyme and will be able to provide a string of rhyming words, but inability to do this does not prevent moving on to Phase Two as these speaking and listening activities continue. (See Appendix 3: Assessment).

The purpose of this phase is to teach at least 19 letters, and move children on from oral blending and segmentation to blending and segmenting with letters. By the end of the phase many children should be able to read some VC and CVC words and to spell them either using magnetic letters or by writing the letters on paper or on whiteboards. During the phase they will be introduced to reading two-syllable words and simple captions. They will also learn to read some high-frequency 'tricky' words: the, to, go, no.

The teaching materials in this phase suggest an order for teaching letters and provide a selection of suitable words made up of the letters as they are learned. These words are for using in the activities – practising blending for reading and segmenting for spelling. This is not a list to be worked through slavishly, but to be selected from as needed for an activity.

It must always be remembered that phonics is the step up to word recognition. Automatic reading of all words – decodable and tricky – is the ultimate goal.

Letter progression (one set per week)

Set 1:	s	a	t	p	
Set 2:	i	n	m	d	
Set 3:	g	o	c	k	
Set 4:	ck	e	u	r	
Set 5:	h	b	f, ff	l, ll	ss

Magnetic boards and letters

Magnetic boards and letters are very effective in helping children to identify letter shapes and develop the skills of blending and segmenting. For example, teaching sequences can be demonstrated to an entire teaching group or class on a large magnetic board followed by children working in pairs with a small magnetic board to secure the learning objective. Working in pairs in this way significantly increases opportunities for children to discuss the task in hand and enlarge their understanding. Once children are adept at manipulating magnetic boards and letters they can use them to extend many activities suggested in Phase Two and beyond.

Suggested daily teaching in Phase Two

Sequence of teaching in a discrete phonics session

Introduction
Objectives and criteria for success

Revisit and review

Teach

Practise

Apply

Assess learning against criteria

Revisit and review

- Practise previously learned letters

- Practise oral blending and segmentation

Teach

- Teach a new letter

- Teach blending and/or segmentation with letters (weeks 2 and 3)

- Teach one or two tricky words (week 3 onwards)

Practise

- Practise reading and/or spelling words with the new letter

Apply

- Read or write a caption (with the teacher) using one or more high-frequency words and words containing the new letter (week 3 onwards)

Suggested timetable for Phase Two – discrete teaching

Week 1
- Teach set 1 letters
- Practise the letter(s) and sound(s) learned so far
- Briefly practise oral blending and segmentation

Week 2
- Teach set 2 letters
- Practise all previously learned letters and sounds
- Briefly practise oral blending and segmentation
- Teach blending with letters (blending for reading)
- Practise blending for reading
- Practise blending and reading the high-frequency words is, it, in, at

Week 3
- Teach set 3 letters
- Practise previously learned letters and sounds
- Briefly practise oral blending and segmentation
- Practise blending with letters (reading words)
- Teach segmentation for spelling
- Teach blending and reading the high-frequency word and
- Demonstrate reading captions using words with sets 1 and 2 letters and and

Week 4
- Teach **ck**, explain its use at the end of words and practise reading words ending in **ck**
- Teach the three other set 4 letters
- Practise previously learned letters and sounds
- Briefly practise oral blending and segmentation
- Practise blending to read words
- Practise segmentation to spell words
- Teach reading the tricky words to and the
- Support children in reading captions using sets 1–4 letters and the, to and and
- Demonstrate spelling captions using sets 1–4 letters and and

Week 5
- Teach set 5 letters and sounds
- Explain **ff**, **ll** and **ss** at the end of words
- Practise previously learned letters and sounds
- Practise blending to read words
- Practise segmentation to spell words
- Teach reading tricky words no, go, I
- Support children in reading captions using sets 1–5 letters and no, go, I, the, to
- Demonstrate spelling captions using sets 1–5 letters and and, to and the

Week 6
- Revise all the letters and sounds taught so far
- Continue to support children in reading words and captions

Teaching sets 1–5 letters

Teaching a letter

Three-part example session for teaching the letter s

Purpose

■ To learn to say a discrete phoneme, recognise and write the letter that represents that phoneme

Resources

■ Fabric snake

■ Card showing, on one side, a picture of a snake (mnemonic) in the shape of the letter **s** with the letter **s** superimposed in black on the snake; on the other side, the letter **s**

■ Small whiteboards, pens and wipes or paper and pencils

Procedure

Hear it and say it

1. Display the picture of a snake.

2. Make a hissing noise as you produce a snake from behind your back; show the children the **sssssnake** and make the snake into an **s** shape.

3. Weave your hand like a snake making an **s** shape, encouraging the children to do the same.

4. If any children in the room have names with the **s** sound in them, say their names, accentuating the **sssss** (e.g. **Ssssarah, Chrisssssss, Sssssandip**).

5. Do the same with other words (e.g. **ssssand, bussss**) accepting suggestions from the children if they offer, but not asking for them.

See it and say it

1. On the card with the picture of the snake, move your finger down the snake from its mouth, saying **sssss** and saying **sssnake** when you reach its tail.

2. Repeat a number of times, encouraging the children to join in.

3. Write **s** next to the snake and say **sssssssssss**.

4. Ask the children to repeat **sssssssssss**.

Letters and Sounds: Principles and Practice of High Quality Phonics
Primary *National Strategy*

00281-2007BKT-EN

5. Point to the snake and say **sssssnake** and to the **s** and say **sssssssssssss**.

6. Repeat with the children joining in.

7. Put the card behind your back and explain that when you show the snake side of the card, the children should say snake and when you show the **s** side of the card, they should say **s**.

Say it and write it

1. Move your finger slowly down the snake from its mouth, this time saying the letter formation patter: *Round the snake's head, slide down his back and round his tail*.

2. Repeat a couple of times.

3. Repeat a couple more times with the children joining in the patter as they watch you.

4. Ask the children to put their 'writing finger' or 'pencil' in the air and follow you in making an **s** shape, also saying the patter. Repeat a couple of times.

5. Ask them to do the same again, either tracing **s** in front of them on the carpet or sitting in a line and tracing **s** on the back of the child in front.

6. Finally, the children write **s** on whiteboards or paper at tables.

Practising letter recognition (for reading) and recall (for spelling)

As soon as the first three letters (**s**, **a**, **t**) are learned, play games to give the children lots of practice in recognising and recalling the letters quickly. Fast recognition of letters is very important for reading, and recall for spelling. A toy could 'help' you by doing the pointing (recognition) or saying the sounds of the letters (recall).

Recognition (for reading)

Flashcards

Purpose

■ To say as quickly as possible the correct sound when a letter is displayed

Resources

■ Set of A4 size cards with a letter on one side and its mnemonic on the other (e.g. the letter **s** on one side and a picture of a snake shaped like an **s** on the other)

Procedure

1. Hold up the letter cards the children have learned, one at a time.

2. Ask the children, in chorus, to say the letter-sound (with the action if used).

3. If the children do not respond, turn the card over to show the mnemonic.

4. Sometimes you could ask the children to say the letter-sounds in a particular way (e.g. happy, sad, bossy or timid – mood sounds).

5. As the children become familiar with the letters, increase the speed of presentation so that the children learn to respond quickly.

Interactive whiteboard variation

Resources

■ Interactive whiteboard with large letters stacked up one behind the other

Procedure

1. Reveal letters one by one by 'pulling' them across with your finger, gradually speeding up.

Frieze

Resources

■ Frieze of letters

■ Pointing stick/hand

Procedure

1. Ask the children to tell you the sounds of the letters as you point to the letters at random.

2. As the children become familiar with the letters, increase the speed of presentation so that the children learn to respond quickly.

3. Sometimes ask a child to 'be teacher' as this gives children confidence and gives you the opportunity to watch and assess them as they respond.

Interactive whiteboard variation

Resources

■ Interactive whiteboard

Procedure

1. Display the letters the children have learned.

2. Either point to one letter at a time or remotely colour one letter at a time and ask the children to tell you each letter-sound.

Recall (for spelling)

Fans

Purpose

■ To find the correct letter in response to a letter-sound being spoken

Resources

■ Fans with letters from sets 1 and 2 (e.g. **s**, **a**, **t**, **p**, **i**, **n**), one per child or pair of children

Procedure

1. Say a letter-sound and ask the children to find the letter on the fan and leave it at the top, sliding the other letters out of sight.

2. If all the children have fans ask them to check that they have the same answer as their partners. If the children are sharing, they ask their partners whether they agree.

3. Ask the children to hold up their fans for you to see.

Variations

■ The children have two different fans each.

■ The children work in pairs with three different fans.

Quickwrite letters

Resources

■ Small whiteboards, pens and wipes for each child or pair of children

Procedure

1. Say a letter-sound (with the mnemonic and action if necessary) and ask the children to write it, saying the letter formation patter as they do so.

2. If the children are sharing a whiteboard both write, one after the other.

Practising oral blending and segmentation

These blending and segmentation skills were introduced in Phase One with a soft toy that 'could only speak and understand sound-talk'. Blending and segmenting are the inverse of one another and need regular practice during Phase Two but blending and segmentation with letters should replace oral segmentation and blending as soon as possible.

Practising oral blending

Purpose

■ To give children oral experience of blending phonemes into words so that they are already familiar with the blending process when they start to read words made from the letter-sounds they are being taught

From time to time during the day, say some words in 'sound-talk'. For example:

■ sound-talk a word in an instruction (e.g. *Give yourselves a **p-a-t** on the back*);

■ say some of the children's names in sound-talk when sending them to an activity or out to play.

Georgie's gym

Resources

■ Soft toy

Procedure

Use the soft toy to give instructions, 'Georgie says', for example:

1. Stand **u-p**.

2. Put your hands on your **kn-ee-s**, on your **f-ee-t**.

3. Put your finger on your **n-o-se**.

4. Bend one arm round your **b-a-ck**.

5. Wiggle your…

What's missing?

Resources

- Set of any six CVC objects from the role-play area (e.g. hospital: soap, pen, chart, book, mug)

- List of nine words for the teacher to read out, which includes the six objects and three additional items (e.g. bed, sheet, pill)

- Soft toy (optional)

Procedure

1. Pretext: you (or the soft toy) need to check that you have collected together all the items you need, which are written on your list.

2. Display the six objects.

3. Say one of the words on the list using sound-talk, ask the children to repeat it and then tell their partners what it is.

4. The children look at the items in front of them to see if the object is there.

Practising oral segmentation

Purpose

■ To give children experience of breaking words up orally into their constituent phonemes so that they can use their knowledge of letter-sounds to spell words

Resources

■ Soft toy

■ List of words, pictures or objects

Procedure

1. Pretext: the toy is deciding what to put into his picnic basket and the children are asked to help him decide, but he only understands sound-talk.

2. Ask the children whether he will need an item (e.g. jam).

3. If the children think he will, ask them to say the word and then tell the toy in sound-talk: jam, **j-a-m**. The children may benefit from making some action with their hands or arms in time to the sound-talk.

4. Continue with a series of both suitable and unsuitable items (e.g. cheese, mud, cake, nuts, juice, coal, ham, rolls, soap, mugs, mouse).

Teaching and practising blending for reading VC and CVC words

Blending for reading is a combination of letter recognition and oral blending (see *Notes of Guidance for Practitioners and Teachers*, pages 10–11, for an explanation). Some children need a lot of practice before they grasp CVC blending.

Teaching blending for reading

Sound buttons

Resources

- Words on cards or on magnetic or an interactive whiteboard with sound buttons as illustrated

at

Procedure

This sequence of suggestions will require building over a few days.

1. Display a VC word (e.g. *it*, *at*) and point to or draw a sound button under each letter.

2. Sound-talk and then tell the children the word.

3. Repeat, but ask the children to tell their partners the word after you have sound-talked it.

4. Repeat 2 and 3 with a CVC word.

5. Repeat 4 with a couple more words.

6. Display another word, ask the children to sound-talk it with you and then say the word to their partners.

7. Repeat 6 with a couple more words.

8. Display another word and ask the children to sound-talk it in chorus, wait for you to repeat the sounds after them and then say the word to their partners.

9. Repeat 8 with more words.

10. Finally, display another word and ask the children to sound-talk the word in chorus and then, without your repeating the sounds, say the word to their partners.

11. Repeat 10 with more words.

This procedure can be 'wrapped up' in a playful manner by using a toy or a game but the purpose of blending for reading should not be eclipsed as the prime motive for the children's learning (see 'Practising blending for reading' on page 59).

Practising blending for reading

What's in the box?

Resources

- Set of word cards (e.g. words containing sets 1 and 2 letters – see 'Bank of suggested words for practising reading and spelling' on page 69)

- Set of objects or pictures corresponding to the word cards, hidden in a box

- Soft toy (optional)

Procedure

1. Display a word card (e.g. map).

2. Go through the letter recognition and blending process appropriate to the children's development (see 'Teaching blending for reading' on page 58).

3. Ask the toy or a child to find the object or picture in the box.

Variation 1 (to additionally develop vocabulary)

1. Attach some pictures to the whiteboard using reusable sticky pads or magnets or display some objects.

2. Display a word card.

3. Go through the letter recognition and blending process appropriate to the children's development.

4. Ask a child to place the word card next to the corresponding picture or object.

Variation 2 (when the children are becoming confident blenders)

1. The children sit in two lines opposite one another.

2. Give the children in one line an object or picture and the children in the other line a word card.

3. The children with the word cards read their words and the children with objects or pictures sound-talk the name of their object or picture to the child sitting next to them.

4. Ask the children to hold up their words and objects or pictures so the children sitting in the line opposite can see them.

5. Ask the children with word cards to stand up and go across to the child in the line opposite who has the corresponding object or picture.

6. All the children check that they have the right match.

Small group with adult

The following activities can be played without an adult present but when they are completed the children seek out an adult to check their decisions.

Matching words and pictures

(Resources as above).

Procedure

1. Lay out the word cards and picture cards on a table.

2. Ask the children to match the word cards to the pictures.

Buried treasure

Purpose

■ To motivate children to read the words and so gain valuable reading practice

Resources

■ About eight cards, shaped and coloured like gold coins, with words and nonsense words on them made up from letters the children have been learning (e.g. mop, cat, man, mip, pon, mon), buried in the sand tray

■ Containers representing a treasure chest and a waste bin, or pictures of a treasure chest and a waste bin on large sheets of paper, placed flat on a table

Procedure

Ask the children to sort the coins into the treasure chest and the waste bin, putting the coins with proper words on them (e.g. man) in the treasure chest and those with meaningless words (e.g. mon) in the waste bin.

When children have blended the sounds to read a word a number of times on different occasions, either overtly or under their breath, they will begin to read the word 'automatically' without needing to blend.

Teaching and practising segmenting VC and CVC words for spelling

Teaching segmentation for spelling is a combination of oral segmentation and letter recall (see *Notes of Guidance for Practitioners and Teachers*, pages 10–11, for an explanation). Some children need a lot of practice before they grasp CVC segmentation.

Teaching segmentation

Phoneme frame

Resources

■ Large two-phoneme or three-phoneme frame drawn on a magnetic or interactive whiteboard as illustrated

■ Selection of magnetic letters (e.g. sets 1 and 2 letters) displayed on a whiteboard

■ List of words (visible only to the teacher)

■ Small phoneme frames, each with a selection of magnetic letters, or six-letter fans, one per child or pair of children

■ Soft toy (optional)

Procedure

This sequence of suggestions will require building over a few days. Children should be able to spell VC words before moving on to spell CVC words.

1. Say a VC word (e.g. **at**) and then say it in sound-talk.

2. Say another VC word (e.g. **it**) and ask the children to tell their partners what it would be in sound-talk.

3. Demonstrate finding the letter **i** from the selection of magnetic letters and put it in the first square on phoneme frame and the letter **t** in the second square, sound-talk **i-t** and then say **it**.

4. Say another VC word (e.g. **in**) and ask the children to tell their partners what it would be in sound-talk.

5. Ask the children to tell you what to put in the first square in the phoneme frame and then in the second.

6. Ask the children to make the word on their own phoneme frames or fans.

7. If all the children have frames or fans, ask them to check that they have the same answer as their partners. If the children are sharing, they ask their partners whether they agree.

8. Ask the children to hold up their frames or fans for you to see.

9. Repeat 4–8 with another VC word (e.g. **an**).

10. Repeat 1–8 with three-phoneme (CVC) words containing the selection of letters.

See 'Bank of suggested words for practising reading and spelling' (on page 69).

This procedure can also be 'wrapped up' in a playful manner by 'helping a toy' to write words.

Practising segmentation

Phoneme frame

See 'Teaching and practising VC and CVC words for spelling' (on page 61).

Quickwrite words

Resources

- Large three-phoneme frame drawn on a magnetic whiteboard

- Display of letters required for words

- List of CVC words (visible only to the teacher)

- Hand-held phoneme frames on whiteboards, pens and wipes, one per child or pair of children

Procedure

1. Say a CVC word and, holding up three fingers, sound-talk it, pointing to a finger at a time for each phoneme.

2. Ask the children to do the same and watch to check that they are correct.

3. Holding up the three fingers on one hand, write the letters of the word in the phoneme frame, demonstrating how to refer to the letter display to recall a letter.

4. Ask the children to write the word in their phoneme frames.

5. Say another word and ask the children to sound-talk it to their partners using their fingers.

6. Ask them to sound-talk it in chorus for you to write it.

7. Repeat 5 and 6 but leave the last letter of the word for the children to write on their own.

8. Ask them to sound-talk (with fingers) and write more words you say.

Full circle

Resources

- List of words (sat, sit, sip, tip, tap, sap, sat), magnetic whiteboards and letters (**s**, **a**, **t**, **p**, **i**), one per pair of children

- List of words (pin, pit, sit, sat, pat, pan, pin), magnetic whiteboards and letters (**s**, **a**, **t**, **p**, **i**, **n**), one per pair of children

- List of words (pot, pod, pad, sad, mad, mat, pat, pot), magnetic whiteboards and letters (**p**, **t**, **d**, **m**, **s**, **o**, **a**), one per pair of children

- List of words (cat, can, man, map, mop, cop, cap, cat), magnetic whiteboards and letters (**c**, **t**, **n**, **m**, **p**, **a**, **o**), one per pair of children

- List of words (leg, peg, pet, pat, rat, ran, rag, lag, leg), magnetic whiteboards and letters (**l**, **g**, **p**, **t**, **r**, **n**, **e**, **a**), one per pair of children

- List of words (run, bun, but, bit, hit, him, dim, din, sin, sun, run), magnetic whiteboards and letters (**r**, **n**, **b**, **t**, **h**, **m**, **s**, **d**, **i**, **u**), one per pair of children

Procedure

1. Give pairs of children a magnetic whiteboard and the appropriate letters for one game of 'Full circle'.

2. Say the first word (e.g. sat) and ask the children to make it with their letters.

3. Write sat on the whiteboard and explain that the children are going to keep changing letters to make lots of words and that when they make sat again, they may call out *Full circle*.

4. Leave sat written on the whiteboard throughout the activity.

5. Ask the children to sound-talk sat and then sit and then to change sat into sit on their magnetic whiteboards.

6. Ask them to sound-talk and blend the word to check that it is correct.

7. Repeat with each word in the list until the first word comes round again and then say *Full circle* with the children.

 Letters and Sounds: Principles and Practice of High Quality Phonics
Primary *National Strategy*

00281-2007BKT-EN
© Crown copyright 2007

Teaching and practising high-frequency (common) words

There are 100 common words that recur frequently in much of the written material young children read and that they need when they write. Most of these are decodable, by sounding and blending, assuming the grapheme–phoneme correspondences are known, but only 26 of the high-frequency words are decodable by the end of Phase Two. Reading a group of these words each day, by applying grapheme–phoneme knowledge as it is acquired, will help children recognise them quickly. However, in order to read simple captions it is necessary also to know some words that have unusual or untaught GPCs ('tricky' words) and these need to be learned (see *Notes of Guidance for Practitioners and Teachers*, page 15).

Teaching 'tricky' high-frequency words

the   to   I   go   no

Resources

- Caption containing the tricky word to be learned (see 'Bank of suggested captions for practising reading' on page 71)

Procedure

1. Explain that there are some words that have one, or sometimes two, tricky letters.

2. Read the caption, pointing to each word, then point to the word to be learned and read it again.

3. Write the word on the whiteboard.

4. Sound-talk the word and repeat putting sound lines and buttons (as illustrated above) under each phoneme and blending them to read the word.

5. Discuss the tricky bit of the word where the letters do not correspond to the sounds the children know (e.g. in **go**, the last letter does not represent the same sound as the children know in **dog**).

6. Read the word a couple more times and refer to it regularly throughout the day so that by the end of the day the children can read the word straight away without sounding out.

Practising reading high-frequency words

Children should be given lots of practice with sounding and blending the 26 decodable high-frequency words so that they will be able to read them 'automatically' as soon as possible. They also need practice with reading the five tricky words, paying attention to any known letter–sound correspondences.

Resources

■ Between five and eight high-frequency words, including decodable and tricky words, written on individual cards

Procedure

1. Display a word card.

2. Point to each letter in the word as the children sound-talk the letters (as far as is possible with tricky words) and read the word.

3. Say a sentence using the word, slightly emphasising the word.

4. Repeat 1–3 with each word card.

5. Display each word again, and repeat the procedure more quickly but without giving a sentence.

6. Repeat once more, asking the children to say the word without sounding it out.

Give the children a caption incorporating the high-frequency words to read at home.

Introducing two-syllable words for reading

Resources

■ Short list of two-syllable words

Procedure

1. Write a two-syllable word on the whiteboard making a slash between the two syllables (e.g. sun/set).

2. Sound-talk the first syllable and blend it: **s-u-n** sun.

3. Sound-talk the second syllable and blend it: **s-e-t** set.

4. Say both syllables: sunset.

5. Repeat and ask the children to join in.

6. Repeat with another word.

Teaching reading and writing captions

Reading captions

Matching

Resources

- Three pictures and a caption for one of the pictures

Procedure

1. Display the caption.

2. Sound-talk and read the first word (e.g. **p-a-t** pat).

3. Ask the children to repeat after you or join in with you, depending on their progress.

4. After sound-talking (if necessary) and reading the second word, say both words (e.g. a, pat a).

5. Continue with the next word (e.g. **d-o-g** dog, pat a dog).

6. Display the pictures and ask the children which picture the caption belongs to.

Note: As children get more practice with the high-frequency words, it should not be necessary to continue sound-talking them.

Shared reading

When reading a shared text to the children for the purpose of familiarising them with print conventions (direction, one-to-one word correspondence, etc.) locate occasional VC and CVC words comprising the letters the children have learned, sound-talk and blend them.

Writing captions

Demonstration writing

Resources

■ Picture of subjects that have VC and CVC names (e.g. a cat sitting in a hat)

Procedure

1. Display and discuss the picture.

2. Ask the children to help you write a caption for the picture (e.g. a cat in a hat).

3. Ask them to say the caption all together a couple of times and then say it again to their partners.

4. Ask them to say it again all together two or three times.

5. Ask the children to tell you the first word.

6. Ask what letters are needed and write it.

7. Remind the children that a space is needed between words and put a mark where the next word will start.

8. Ask the children to say the caption again.

9. Ask for the next word and ask what letters are needed.

10. Repeat for each word.

Shared writing

When writing in front of the children, take the occasional opportunity to ask them to help you spell words by telling you which letters to write.

Independent writing

When the children are writing, for example in role-play areas, their letter awareness along with their ability to segment will allow them to make a good attempt at writing many of the words they wish to use. Even though some of their spellings may be inaccurate, the experience gives them further practice in segmentation and, even more importantly, gives them experience in composition and helps them see themselves as writers.

Assessment

(See *Notes of Guidance for Practitioners and Teachers*, page 16.)

By the end of Phase Two children should:

- give the sound when shown any Phase Two letter, securing first the starter letters **s**, **a**, **t**, **p**, **i**, **n**;

- find any Phase Two letter, from a display, when given the sound;

- be able to orally blend and segment CVC words;

- be able to blend and segment in order to read and spell (using magnetic letters) VC words such as if, am, on, up and 'silly names' such as ip, ug and ock;

- be able to read the five tricky words the, to, I, no, go.

Some children will not have fully grasped CVC blending and segmentation but may know all the Phase Two letters. CVC blending and segmentation continues throughout Phase Three so children can progress to the next stage even if they have not mastered CVC blending.

Writing

Children's capacity to write letters will depend on their physical maturity and the teaching approach taken to letter formation. Some children will be able to write all the letters in pencil, correctly formed. Most children should be able to form the letters correctly in the air, in sand or using a paint brush and should be able to control a pencil sufficiently well to write letters such as **l**, **t**, **i** well and **h**, **n** and **m** reasonably well.

Bank of suggested words for practising reading and spelling

The words in this section are made up from the letters taught for use in blending for reading and segmentation for spelling. These lists are not for working through slavishly but to be selected from as needed for an activity (words in italics are from the list of 100 high-frequency words).

Words using set 1 GPC

For ** see next page

at
sat
pat
tap
sap
[a*, as**]

Words using sets 1 and 2 GPCs

(+i)	(+n)	(+m)	(+d)
it	*an*	am	*dad*
is**	*in*	man	sad
sit	nip	mam	dim
sat	pan	mat	dip
pit	pin	map	din
tip	tin	Pam	did
pip	tan	Tim	Sid
sip	nap	Sam	*and*

Words using sets 1–3 GPCs

(+g)	(+o)	(+c)	(+k)
tag	*got*	*can*	kid
gag	*on*	cot	kit
gig	*not*	cop	Kim
gap	pot	cap	Ken
nag	top	cat	
sag	dog	cod	
gas	pop		
pig	God		
dig	Mog		

Words using sets 1–4 GPCs

(+ck)	(+e)	(+u)	(+r)
kick	*get*	*up*	rim
sock	pet	*mum*	rip
sack	ten	run	ram
dock	net	mug	rat
pick	pen	cup	rag
sick	peg	sun	rug
pack	met	tuck	rot
ticket	men	mud	rocket
pocket	neck	sunset	carrot

Teach that 'ck' together stands for the same sound as 'c' and 'k' separately – ck never comes at the beginning of a word, but often comes at the end or near the end.

*The indefinite article 'a' is normally pronounced as a schwa, but this is close enough to the /a/ sound to be manageable.

Words using sets 1–5 letters

(+h)	(+b)	(+f and ff)	(+l and ll)	(+ss)
had	*but*	*of**	lap	ass
him	*big*	*if*	let	less
*his***	*back*	*off*	leg	hiss
hot	bet	fit	lot	mass
hut	bad	fin	lit	mess
hop	bag	fun	bell	boss
hum	bed	fig	fill	fuss
hit	bud	fog	doll	hiss
hat	beg	puff	tell	pass (*north*)
has **	bug	huff	sell	kiss
hack	bun	cuff	Bill	Tess
hug	bus	fan	Nell	fusspot
	Ben	fat	dull	
	bat		laptop	
	bit			
	bucket			
	beckon			
	rabbit			

When the letters **l**, **s** and **f** double at the ends of some words and **c** is joined by **k**, it is a good idea to draw a line underneath both letters to show that they represent one phoneme (e.g. hi<u>ll</u>, pi<u>ck</u>) when providing words and captions for reading, and encourage children to do so in their writing.

The sounds represented by **f in of, and by **s** in as, is, has and his should also not cause problems at this stage, especially as children will not learn the letters **v** and **z** until several weeks later. Note that /**f**/ is articulated in the same way as /**v**/, and /**s**/ as /**z**/, apart from the fact that /**f**/ and /**s**/ are unvoiced and /**v**/ and /**z**/ are voiced.

Bank of suggested captions for practising reading

Captions with sets 1–4 words

pat a dog	dad and nan
a cat in a hat	a nap in a cot
a sad man	a kid in a cap
a pin on a map	a tin can
pots and pans	cats and dogs

Captions with sets 1–4 words + *to, the*

a red rug	rats on a sack
get to the top	a pup in the mud
socks on a mat	run to the den
a cap on a peg	mugs and cups
a run in the sun	an egg in an egg cup

Captions, instructions and signs with sets 1–5 words + *to, the, no, go*

a hug and a kiss	a cat on a bed
on top of the rock	to the top of the hill
a bag of nuts	get off the bus
to huff and puff	no lid on the pan
go to the log hut	pack a pen in a bag
a hot hob	a doll in a cot
sit back to back	a cat and a big fat rat
a duck and a hen	

The captions are included to provide a bridge between the reading of single words and the reading of books. They enable children to use and apply their decoding skills on simple material fully compatible with the word-reading level they have reached. This helps them to gain confidence and begin to read simple books.

Letters and sounds: **Phase Three**

Phase Three

(up to 12 weeks)

Contents

Key

This icon indicates that the activity
can be viewed on the DVD.

Letters and Sounds: Principles and Practice of High Quality Phonics
Primary *National Strategy*

00281-2007BKT-EN

Summary

Children entering Phase Three will know around 19 letters and be able to blend phonemes to read VC words and segment VC words to spell. While many children will be able to read and spell CVC words, they all should be able to blend and segment CVC words orally. (See Appendix 3: Assessment).

The purpose of this phase is to teach another 25 graphemes, most of them comprising two letters (e.g. **oa**), so the children can represent each of about 42 phonemes by a grapheme (the additional phoneme /**zh**/ found in the word **vision** will be taught at Phase Five). Children also continue to practise CVC blending and segmentation in this phase and will apply their knowledge of blending and segmenting to reading and spelling simple two-syllable words and captions. They will learn letter names during this phase, learn to read some more tricky words and also begin to learn to spell some of these words.

The teaching materials in this phase suggest an order for teaching letters and provide a selection of suitable words made up of the letters as they are learned and captions and sentences made up of the words. They are for using in the activities – practising blending for reading and segmenting for spelling. These are not lists to be worked through slavishly but to be selected from as needed for an activity.

It must always be remembered that phonics is the step up to word recognition. Automatic reading of all words – decodable and tricky – is the ultimate goal.

Letters

Set 6:	j	v	w	x*

Set 7:	y	z, zz	qu*

*The sounds traditionally taught for the letters **x** and **qu** (/**ks**/ and /**kw**/) are both two phonemes, but children do not need to be taught this, at this stage as it does not affect how the letters are used.

Graphemes	Sample words	Graphemes	Sample words
ch	chip	ar	farm
sh	shop	or	for
th	thin/then	ur	hurt
ng	ring	ow	cow
ai	rain	oi	coin
ee	feet	ear	dear
igh	night	air	fair
oa	boat	ure	sure
oo	boot/look	er	corner

Suggested daily teaching in Phase Three

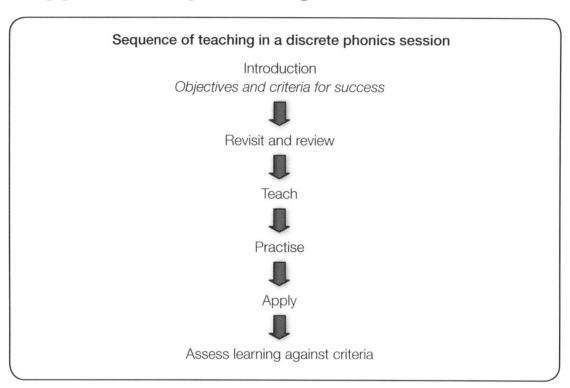

Sequence of teaching in a discrete phonics session

Introduction
Objectives and criteria for success

⬇

Revisit and review

⬇

Teach

⬇

Practise

⬇

Apply

⬇

Assess learning against criteria

Revisit and review

■ Practise previously learned letters or graphemes

Teach

■ Teach new graphemes

■ Teach one or two tricky words

Practise

■ Practise blending and reading words with a new GPC

■ Practise segmenting and spelling words with a new GPC

Apply

■ Read or write a caption or sentence using one or more tricky words and words containing the graphemes

Suggested timetable for Phase Three
– discrete teaching

Week 1
- Practise previously learned letters and sounds
- Teach set 6 letters and sounds
- Learn an alphabet song
- Practise blending for reading
- Practise segmentation for spelling
- Practise reading high-frequency words
- Read sentences using sets 1–6 letters and the tricky words no, go, I, the, to

Week 2
- Practise previously learned letters and sounds
- Teach set 7 letters and sounds
- Point to the letters in the alphabet while singing the alphabet song
- Practise blending for reading
- Practise segmentation for spelling
- Teach reading the tricky words he, she
- Practise reading and spelling high-frequency words
- Teach spelling the tricky words the and to
- Practise reading captions and sentences with sets 1–7 letters and he, she, no, go, I, the, to

Week 3
- Practise previously learned GPCs
- Teach the four consonant digraphs
- Point to the letters in the alphabet while singing the alphabet song
- Practise blending for reading
- Practise segmentation for spelling
- Teach reading the tricky words we, me, be
- Practise reading and spelling high-frequency words
- Practise reading two-syllable words
- Practise reading captions and sentences
- Practise writing captions and sentences

Week 4
- Practise previously learned GPCs
- Teach four of the vowel digraphs
- Point to the letters in the alphabet while singing the alphabet song
- Practise blending for reading
- Practise segmentation for spelling
- Teach reading the tricky word was
- Teach spelling the tricky words no and go
- Practise reading and spelling high-frequency words
- Practise reading two-syllable words
- Practise reading captions and sentences
- Practise writing captions and sentences

Week 5
- Practise previously learned GPCs
- Teach four more vowel digraphs
- Point to the letters in the alphabet while singing the alphabet song

– Practise blending for reading
– Practise segmentation for spelling
– Teach reading the tricky word **my**
– Practise reading and spelling high-frequency words
– Teach spelling two-syllable words
– Practise reading captions and sentences
– Practise writing captions and sentences

Week 6
– Practise previously learned GPCs
– Teach four more vowel digraphs
– Practise letter names
– Practise blending for reading
– Practise segmentation for spelling
– Teach reading the tricky word **you**
– Practise reading and spelling high-frequency words
– Practise spelling two-syllable words
– Practise reading captions and sentences
– Practise writing captions and sentences

Week 7
– Practise previously learned GPCs
– Teach four more vowel digraphs
– Practise letter names
– Practise blending for reading
– Practise segmentation for spelling
– Teach reading the tricky word **they**
– Practise reading and spelling high-frequency words
– Practise spelling two-syllable words
– Practise reading captions and sentences
– Practise writing captions and sentences

Week 8
– Practise all GPCs
– Practise letter names
– Practise blending for reading
– Practise segmentation for spelling
– Teach reading the tricky word **her**
– Practise reading and spelling high-frequency words
– Practise spelling two-syllable words
– Practise reading captions and sentences
– Practise writing captions and sentences

Week 9
– Practise all GPCs
– Practise letter names
– Practise blending for reading
– Practise segmentation for spelling
– Teach reading the tricky word **all**
– Practise reading and spelling high-frequency words
– Practise spelling two-syllable words
– Practise reading captions and sentences
– Practise writing captions and sentences

Letters and Sounds: Principles and Practice of High Quality Phonics
Primary *National Strategy*

00281-2007BKT-EN

Week 10 – Practise all GPCs
– Practise letter names
– Practise blending for reading
– Practise segmentation for spelling
– Teach reading the tricky word are
– Practise reading and spelling words
– Practise spelling two-syllable high-frequency words
– Practise reading captions and sentences
– Practise writing captions and sentences

Weeks 11–12 – More consolidation if necessary, or move on to Phase Four.

Teaching sets 6 and 7 letters

Teaching a letter

Three-part example session for teaching the letter y

Purpose

■ To learn to say a discrete phoneme, recognise and write the letter that represents that phoneme

Resources

■ Yoyo

■ Card showing, on one side, a picture of a yoyo (mnemonic) with the letter *y* superimposed in black on the yoyo; on the other side, the letter *y*

■ Small whiteboards, pens and wipes or paper and pencils for each child

Procedure

Hear it and say it

1. Make a **y-y-y-y** noise as you produce a yoyo from behind your back.

2. Continue to say **y** in time to the movement of the yoyo.

3. Ask the children to stand up and pretend to play with a yoyo, saying **y** each time the yoyo goes down.

4. If any children in the room have names with the y sound in them, say their names, accentuating the **y** (e.g. **YYY**Yolande, **YYY**Yasmine).

5. Do the same with other words (e.g. yes, yellow, accepting suggestions from the children if they offer them.

See it and say it

1. Display the picture of a yoyo.

2. Ask the children to repeat **y-y-y-yoyo**.

3. Move your finger down and round the yoyo and down the string, saying **y-y-y** and saying **yoyo** when you reach the curled bit of the string.

4. Repeat a number of times, encouraging the children to join in.

5. Write **y** next to the yoyo and say **y-y-y-y-y-y**.

6. Ask the children to repeat **y-y-y-y-y-y**.

7. Point to the yoyo and say **yoyo** and to the **y** and say **y-y-y-y-y-y**.

8. Repeat with the children joining in.

9. Put the card behind your back. Then show the yoyo side of the card and ask the children to say **yoyo**; show the **y** side of the card and the children say **y-y-y-y-y-y**. Make it into a game, sometimes showing the **y** and sometimes the **yoyo**.

Say it and write it

1. Move your finger slowly down and round the yoyo, and down and round the string, this time saying the letter formation patter: *Down and round the yoyo, down and round the string.*

2. Repeat a couple of times.

3. Repeat a couple more times with the children joining in the patter as they watch you.

4. Ask the children to put their 'writing finger' or 'pencil' in the air and follow you, also saying the patter. Repeat a couple of times.

5. Ask them to do the same again, either tracing **y** in front of them on the carpet or sitting in a line and tracing the letter on the back of the child in front.

6. Ask them to hold up their hands and write **y** on the palms of their hands.

7. Finally, the children write **y** on whiteboards or paper at tables.

In teaching the remaining sets 6 and 7 letters:

■ relate **zz** to **ff**, **ll**, and **ss**;

■ explain about **q** always needing **u** after it in English words.

Teaching letter names (if not already taught)

See *Notes of Guidance for Practitioners and Teachers* page 15 for the rationale for teaching and using letter names.

Alphabet song

Resources

- Alphabet song

- Alphabet frieze including lower and upper case letters (or one frieze for each case)

- Selection of toy animals or pictures of animals

Procedure (gradually over a period of two or three weeks)

1. Teach the alphabet song and sing it every day for a week.

2. Display two or three animals (or pictures of animals) and ask the children to indicate which is the cat, the dog, the cow, etc. and then what sound each one makes: meow, woof, moo, etc.

3. Reiterate that one of the animals is a cat and it makes the sound meow.

4. Display a letter (e.g. **t**) and tell the children that it is a **t** (say its name) and stands for the sound /**t**/ (say its sound).

5. Display another letter (e.g. **m**) telling the children what it is. Ask them what sound it stands for (as they already know the sounds of the letters).

6. Display the alphabet frieze and point to the letters as the children sing the alphabet.

7. Continue singing the alphabet daily and pointing to the letters until you are satisfied that all the children know the letter names.

8. Pick out a few letters each day and connect the names with the sounds of the letter.

Introducing and teaching two-letter and three-letter GPCs

Two-part example session for teaching sh

Resources

- **sh** card

- **sh** words

Procedure

Hear it and say it

1. Say the grapheme sound with its mnemonic (e.g. putting your fingers to your lips as though quietening everyone).

2. Invite the children to join in.

3. If any children in the room have names with the **sh** sound in them, say their names, accentuating the **shshshshsh** (e.g. **ShshShona**, **Mishshsha**). If Charlene offers her name, accept it and leave the explanation of the letters until 'See it and say it' below.

4. Do the same with other words (e.g. **shsheep**, **bushsh**, accepting suggestions from the children if they offer them.

See it and say it

1. Display **sh** and explain that this sound needs two letters that the children already know and that to show that two letters stand for one sound we draw a line under them. (Now is the time to tell Charlene that her name certainly does start with /**sh**/ but that it has a different spelling.)

2. Recall that the children have already seen two letters being used in the recently learned **q**, which always has a **u** after it, and also **ck** and the double letters **ll**, **zz**, **ff** and **ss** at the ends of some words.

3. Write some **sh** words on the whiteboard and others as foils (e.g. **shut**, **fish**, **shop**, **dash**, **wishes**, **shell**, **rushed**, **hiss**, **stop**, **such**).

4. Ask six children to come to the whiteboard and one a time to find the word with a **sh** grapheme and underline the grapheme.

Teaching two-letter and three-letter GPCs

Continue to teach mnemonics for Phase Three GPCs.

Practising grapheme recognition (for reading) and recall (for spelling)

Recognition (for reading)

Flashcards

Purpose

- To say as quickly as possible the correct sound when a grapheme is displayed

Resources

- Set of A4 size cards with a grapheme on one side and its mnemonic on the other (e.g. **sh** on one side and a picture of a finger to the mouth on the other)

Procedure

1. Hold up the grapheme cards the children have learned, one at a time.

2. Ask the children, in chorus, to say the sound of the grapheme (with the action, if used).

3. If the children do not respond, turn the card over to show the mnemonic.

4. Increase the speed of presentation so that the children learn to respond quickly.

5. Sometimes you could ask the children to say the sound for the grapheme in a particular way (e.g. happy, sad, bossy, timid – mood sounds).

You could have an identical set of small cards for using through the day with individuals or small groups.

Interactive whiteboard variation

Resources

- Interactive whiteboard with graphemes stacked up one behind the other

Procedure

Reveal graphemes one by one by 'pulling' them across with your finger, gradually speeding up.

Frieze

Resources

- Frieze of graphemes

- Pointing stick/hand

Procedure

1. Point to graphemes, one at a time at random, and ask the children to tell you what they are.

2. Gradually increase the speed of presentation.

3. You could ask a child to 'be teacher' as this gives you the opportunity to watch and assess the children as they respond.

Interactive whiteboard variation

Resources

- Interactive whiteboard

Procedure

1. Display the graphemes the children have learned.

2. Either point to one grapheme at a time or remotely colour one letter at a time.

Recall (for spelling)

Fans

Purpose

- To find the correct grapheme in response to a sound being spoken

Resources

- Fans with a designated set of graphemes (e.g. set 6 and 7 letters **j**, **v**, **w**, **x**, **y**, **z**, **qu**) or Phase Three graphemes (e.g. **ch**, **sh**, **th**, **ng**, **ee**, **ai**), one per child or pair of children

---

Procedure

1. Say the sound of a grapheme and ask the children to find the letter on the fan and leave it at the top, sliding the other letters out of sight.

2. If all the children have fans, ask them to check that they have the same answer as their partners. If the children are sharing, they ask their partners whether they agree.

3. Ask the children to hold up their fans for you to see.

Variations

■ The children have two different fans each.

■ The children work in pairs with three different fans.

Quickwrite letters

Resources

■ Small whiteboards, pens and wipes for each child or pair of children

Procedure

1. Say a set 6 or 7 letter-sound (with the mnemonic and action if necessary) and ask the children to write it, saying the letter formation patter as they do so.

2. If the children are sharing a whiteboard both write, one after the other.

Quickwrite graphemes

(Resources and procedure as for 'Quickwrite letters' above.)

The children have already learned the formation of the letters that combine to form two-letter and three-letter graphemes but many may still need to say the mnemonic patter for the formation as they write. When referring to the individual letters in a grapheme, the children should now be encouraged to use letter names as letters do not stand for their Phase Two sounds when they form part of two-letter and three-letter graphemes.

If you have taught the necessary handwriting joins, it may, at this point, be helpful to teach the easier digraphs as joined units (e.g. *ch*, *th*, *ai*, *ee*, *oa*, *oo*, *ow*, *oi* – see the reference to handwriting in *Notes of Guidance for Practitioners and Teachers*, page 15).

Practising blending for reading

Blending for reading

What's in the box?

Resources

- Set of word cards (e.g. with words containing sets 6 and 7 letters and Phase Three graphemes: see page 100–102 for suggestions)

- Set of objects or pictures corresponding to the word cards, hidden in a box

- Soft toy (optional)

Procedure

1. Display a word card.

2. Go through the grapheme recognition and blending process, placing a sound button below each grapheme, as illustrated. Draw attention to the long sound buttons under the two-letter and three-letter graphemes.

3. Ask the toy or a child to find the corresponding object or picture in the box.

Variation 1 (to additionally develop vocabulary)

1. Attach some pictures to the whiteboard using reusable sticky pads or magnets or display some objects.

2. Display a word card.

3. Go through the grapheme recognition and blending process as above.

4. Ask a child to place the word card next to the corresponding picture or object.

Variation 2 (when children are confident blenders)

1. Children sit in two lines opposite one another.

2. Give the children in one line an object or picture and the children in the other line a word card.

3. Ask the children with word cards to read their words and ask the children with objects or pictures to 'sound-talk' the name of their object or picture to the child sitting next to them.

4. Ask the children to hold up their words and objects or pictures so the children sitting in the line opposite can see them.

 Letters and Sounds: Principles and Practice of High Quality Phonics
Primary *National Strategy*

00281-2007BKT-EN

- Ask the children with word cards to stand up and go across to the child in the line opposite who has the corresponding object or picture.

- All the children check that they have the right match.

Countdown

Resources

- List of Phase Three words

- Sand timer, stop clock or some other way of time-limiting the activity

Procedure

1. Display the list of words, one underneath the other.

2. Explain to the children that the object of this activity is to read as many words as possible before the sand timer or stop clock signals 'Stop'.

3. Start the timer.

4. Call a child's name out and point to the first word.

5. Ask the child to sound-talk the letters and read the word.

6. Repeat with another child reading the next word, until the time runs out.

7. Record the score.

The next time the game is played, the objective is to beat this score.

With less confident children this game could be played with all the children reading the words together.

Sentence substitution

Purpose

- To practise reading words in sentences

Resources

- A number of prepared sentences at the children's current level (see suggestions for sentences for substitution on page 104)

- List of alternative words for each sentence

- Soft toy or puppet (optional)

Procedure

1. Write a sentence on the whiteboard (e.g. **Mark fed the cat**).

2. Ask the children to read the sentence with their partners and raise their hands when they have finished.

3. All the children read it together.

4. Using the toy or puppet, rub out one word in the sentence and substitute a different word (e.g. **Mark fed the dog**).

5. Ask the children to read the sentence with their partners and raise their hands if they think it makes sense.

6. All the children read it together.

7. Continue substituting words to make new sentences – **Mark hid the cat**; **Gail hid the cat**; **Gail hid the moon** – asking the children to read each new sentence to decide whether it makes sense or is ridiculous.

Small group with adult

The following activities can be played without an adult present but when they are completed the children seek out an adult to check.

Matching words and pictures

(Resources as 'What's in the box?' above.)

Procedure

1. Lay out the words and picture cards on a table.

2. Ask the children to match up the words to the pictures.

Buried treasure

Purpose

■ To motivate children to read the words and so gain valuable reading practice

Resources

■ About eight cards, shaped and coloured like gold coins with words and nonsense words on them made up from graphemes the children have been learning (e.g. **jarm**, **win**, **jowd**, **yes**, **wug**, **zip**), buried in the sand tray

■ Containers representing a treasure chest and a waste bin, or pictures of a treasure chest and a waste bin on large sheets of paper, placed flat on the table.

Procedure

1. Ask the children to sort the coins into the treasure chest and the waste bin, putting the coins with proper words on them (e.g. win) in the treasure chest and those with meaningless words (e.g. jowd) in the waste bin.

Sorting

Resources

■ Words, such as the names of farm and zoo animals (e.g. zebra, camel, hen, chimpanzee, panda, cow, yak, sheep, goat, duck)

■ Sorting frame (e.g. farm animals, zoo animals)

Procedure

1. Ask the children to sort the animals by reading the words and putting them into the correct frame.

Practising segmentation for spelling

> ### Segmentation for spelling

Phoneme frame

Resources

■ Large three-phoneme frame drawn on a magnetic whiteboard

■ Selection of magnetic letters or graphemes displayed on the whiteboard (the graphemes should be either custom-made as units or individual letters stuck together using sticky tape e.g. *ch*, *oa*)

■ List of words

■ Small phoneme frames, each with a selection of magnetic letters or six-letter or six-grapheme fans, one per child or pair of children

Procedure

Words made up of sets 6 and 7 letters

1. Say a CVC word (e.g. jam) and then say it in sound-talk.

2. Say another CVC word (e.g. wet) and ask the children to tell their partners what it would be in sound-talk.

3. Demonstrate finding the letter **w** from the selection of magnetic letters and put it into the first square on the phoneme frame, put the letter **e** in the second square, and **t** in the last square. Sound-talk **w**-**e**-**t** and then say wet.

4. Say another CVC word (e.g. zip) and ask the children to tell their partners what it would be in sound-talk.

5. Ask the children to tell you what to put in the first square in the phoneme frame, then in the next and so on.

6. Ask the children to make the word on their own phoneme frames or fans.

7. If all the children have phoneme frames or fans, ask them to check that they have the same answer as their partner. If the children are sharing, they ask their partners whether they agree.

8. Ask the children to hold up their phoneme frames or fans for you to see.

9. Repeat 4–8 with another CVC word.

10. Continue with other CVC words.

Phase Three two-letter and three-letter graphemes

Follow the same procedure as for sets 6 and 7 words. It is important that the graphemes are units, not separate letters.

This procedure can also be 'wrapped up' in a playful manner by helping a toy to write the words.

Quickwrite words

Resources

■ Large three-phoneme frame drawn on a magnetic whiteboard

■ List of words for use by the teacher

■ Display of the magnetic letters required for the words on the list

■ Handheld phoneme frames on whiteboards, pens and wipes, one per child or pair of children

Procedure

1. Say a word and, holding up three fingers, sound-talk it, pointing to a finger at a time for each phoneme.

2. Ask the children to do the same and watch to check that they are correct.

3. Holding up the three fingers on one hand, write the letters of the word in the phoneme frame, consulting the letter display.

4. Ask the children to write the word in their phoneme frames.

5. Say another word and ask the children to sound-talk it to their partners, using their fingers.

6. Ask them to sound-talk it in chorus for you to write it.

7. Repeat 5 and 6 but leave the last letter of the word for the children to write on their own.

8. Ask them to sound-talk (with fingers) and write more words that you say.

Full circle

Resources

When the graphemes sh, ch, th and ng have been learned

- List of words (ship, chip, chin, thin, than, can, cash, rash, rang, ring, rip, ship), magnetic whiteboards and letters (sh, ch, th, ng, p, n, r, c, a, i), for each pair of children

- List of words (song, long, lock, shock, shop, chop, chip, chick, thick, thing, sing, song), magnetic whiteboards and letters (ch, sh, ck, th, ng, s, l, p, i, o), for each pair of children

When the graphemes for the new vowel sounds have been learned

- List of words (car, card, lard, laid, maid, mood, moon, moan, moat, mart, cart, car), magnetic whiteboards and letters (ar, ai, oo, oa, c, d, l, m, n, t), for each pair of children

- List of words (light, right, root, room, roam, road, raid, paid, pain, main, mail, sail, sigh, sight, light), magnetic whiteboards and letters (ai, igh, oo, oa, l, t, r, m, d, p, n, s), for each pair of children

The graphemes should either be custom-made as units or individual letters need to be stuck together using sticky tape (e.g. *ch*, *oa*).

Procedure

1. Give pairs of children a magnetic whiteboard and appropriate letters and graphemes.

2. Say the first word (e.g. ship) and ask the children to make it with their letters.

3. Write ship on the whiteboard and explain to the children that they are going to keep changing letters to make lots of words and that when they make ship again, they may call out Full *circle*; leave ship written on the whiteboard throughout the activity.

4. Ask them to sound-talk **ship** and then **chip** and then to change **ship** into **chip** on their magnetic whiteboards.

5. Ask them to sound-talk and blend the word to check that it is correct.

6. Repeat with each word in the list until the first word comes round again and then say *Full circle* with the children.

Teaching and practising high-frequency (common) words

There are 100 common words that recur frequently in much of the written material young children read and that they need when they write. Most of these are decodable, by sounding and blending, assuming the grapheme–phoneme correspondences are known, but only 26 of the high-frequency words are decodable by the end of Phase Two and a further 12 are decodable by the end of Phase Three. These are **will**, **with**, **that**, **this**, **then**, **them**, **see**, **for**, **now**, **down**, **look** and **too**. Reading a group of these words each day, by applying grapheme-phoneme knowledge as it is acquired, will help children recognise them quickly. However, in order to read simple captions it is necessary also to know some words that have unusual or untaught GPCs, 'tricky' words, and these need to be learned (see *Notes of Guidance for Practitioners and Teachers*, page 15, for an explanation).

Learning to read tricky words

he	she	we	me	be

was	my	you	her	they	all	are

Resources

■ Caption containing the tricky word to be learned.

Procedure

1. Explain that there are some words which have one or sometimes two tricky letters in them.

2. Read the caption, pointing to each word, then point to the word to be learned and read it again.

3. Write the word on the whiteboard.

4. Sound-talk the word, and repeat, putting sound lines and buttons (as illustrated above) under each phoneme and blending them to read the word.

5. Discuss the tricky bit of the word where the letters do not correspond to the sounds the children know (e.g. in **he**, the last letter does not represent the same sound as the children know in **hen**).

6. Read the word a couple more times and refer to it regularly through the day so that by the end of the day the children can read the word straight away, without sounding out.

Note: Emphasise the pattern in the words **he**, **she**, **we**, **me**, **be**. The word **the**, where the letter **e** is pronounced /**ee**/ before a vowel (e.g. **the apple**) is the only other tricky word following this pattern.

Practising high-frequency words

The 12 decodable and 12 tricky high-frequency words need lots of practice in the manner described below so that children will be able to read them 'automatically' as soon as possible.

Resources

■ Between five and eight high-frequency words, including decodable and tricky words, written on individual cards

Procedure

1. Display a word card.

2. Point to each grapheme as the children sound-talk the graphemes (as far as is possible with tricky words) and read the word.

3. Say a sentence using the word, slightly emphasising the word.

4. Repeat 1–3 with each word card.

5. Display each word again and repeat the procedure more quickly but without giving a sentence.

6. Repeat once more, asking the children to say the word without sounding it out.

Give the children a caption or sentence incorporating the high-frequency words to read at home.

Learning to spell and practising tricky words

the　　　　　to　　　　　no　　　　　go　　　　　I

Children should be able to read these words before being expected to learn to spell them.

Resources

■ Whiteboards and pens, preferably one per child

Procedure

1. Write the word to be learned on the whiteboard and check that everyone can read it.

2. Say a sentence using the word.

3. Sound-talk the word raising a finger for each phoneme.

4. Ask the children to do the same.

5. Discuss the letters required for each phoneme, using letter names.

6. Ask the children to trace the shape of the letters on their raised fingers.

7. Rub the word off the whiteboard and ask them to write the word on their whiteboards.

Letters and Sounds: Principles and Practice of High Quality Phonics
Primary *National Strategy*

00281-2007BKT-EN

Teaching reading and spelling two-syllable words

Reading two-syllable words

Resources

- Short list of two-syllable words (for use by the teacher)

Procedure

1. Write a two-syllable word on the whiteboard putting a slash between the two syllables (e.g. **car/park**).

2. Sound-talk the first syllable and blend it: **c-ar car**.

3. Sound-talk the second syllable and blend it: **p-ar-k park**.

4. Say both syllables: **car park**.

5. Repeat and ask the children to join in.

6. Repeat with another word.

Introducing spelling two-syllable words

Resources

- List of words (for use by the teacher)
- Magnetic letters or pens and whiteboards for each child

Procedure

1. Say a word (e.g. **farmyard**) then clap each syllable and ask the children to do the same.

2. Repeat with two or three more words.

3. Clap the first word again and tell the children that the first clap is **farm** and the second is **yard**.

4. Ask the children for the sounds in **farm** and write them, underlining the digraph.

5. Repeat with the second syllable.

6. Read the completed word.

7. Repeat with another word.

8. Ask children to do the same on their whiteboards either by using magnetic letters or by writing.

Practising reading and writing captions and sentences

Reading captions

Matching (with the teacher)

Resources

- Three pictures and a caption or sentence for one of the pictures

Procedure

1. Display the caption or sentence.

2. Sound-talk and read the first word (e.g. **f-i-sh** fish).

3. After sound-talking and reading the second word, say both words (e.g. **a-n-d** and, fish and).

4. Continue with the next word (e.g. **ch-i-p-s** chips, fish and chips).

5. Continue to the end of the caption.

6. Display the pictures.

7. Ask the children which picture the caption belongs to.

8. As children get more practice with the high-frequency words, it should not be necessary to continue sound-talking them.

Matching (independent of the teacher)

Resources

- Set of pictures and corresponding captions or sentences

Procedure

Ask the children to match the pictures and captions.

Drawing

Resources

- Two captions or sentences

- Drawing materials

Procedure

1. Display a caption or sentence.

2. Ask the children to read it with their partners and draw a quick sketch.

3. Repeat with the next caption.

'I can ...' books

Purpose

■ To practise reading

Resources

■ Small zigzag book with 'I can run' (jog, hop, sing, etc.) sentences on one side of each page and a corresponding picture drawn by a child on the other

■ Small four-page empty zigzag books made from half sheets of A4 paper (cut longwise)

■ Action words and phrases (jog, run, hop, bang nails, mop up, cook food, sing songs, fish with bait, chop wood) on cards

■ Paper copies of the action words and phrases

■ Materials for writing, drawing and sticking

Procedure

1. Read the completed zigzag book to the children.

2. Show them the empty books for them to make their own.

3. Display an action word or phrase card, one a time for the children to read.

4. Make available paper copies of the action words and phrases, the empty zigzag books, writing, drawing and sticking materials for the children to make their own zigzag books.

Yes/no questions

Resources

■ A number of prepared questions (see page 104 for suggestions) on card or on an interactive whiteboard

■ Cards with 'yes' on one side and 'no' on the other, one per pair of children

Procedure

1. Give pairs of children yes/no cards.

2. Display a yes/no question for the children to read.

3. Ask them to confer with their partners and decide whether the response is 'yes' or 'no'.

4. Ask the children to show their cards.

5. Invite a pair to read a question.

6. Repeat with another question.

Shared reading

When reading a shared text to the children locate occasional VC, CV and CVC words comprising the letters the children have learned and ask the children to read them.

Writing captions

Demonstration writing

Resources

■ Pictures of subjects that have VC, CV and CVC names (e.g. a shed)

Procedure

1. Display and discuss a picture.

2. Ask the children to help you write a caption for the picture (e.g. **tools in a shed**).

3. Ask them to say the caption all together a couple of times and then again to their partners.

4. Ask them to say it again all together two or three times.

5. Ask the children to tell you the first word.

6. Ask what letters are needed and write the word.

7. Remind the children that a space is needed between words: put a mark where the next word will start.

8. Ask the children to say the caption again.

9. Ask for the next word and ask what letters are needed.

10. Repeat for each word.

Writing sentences

Resources and procedure as for 'Writing captions' but as part of the procedure add to the sentence a capital letter and a full stop.

Shared writing

When writing in front of the children, take the occasional opportunity to ask them to help you spell words by telling you which letters to write.

Independent writing

When children are writing, for example in role-play areas, their growing knowledge of letters along with their ability to segment will allow them to make a good attempt at writing many of the words they wish to use. Even though some of their spellings may be inaccurate, the experience gives them further practice in segmentation and, even more importantly, gives them experience in composition and helps them see themselves as writers. (See the note on invented spelling in *Notes of Guidance for Practitioners and Teachers*, page 13.)

Assessment

(See *Notes of Guidance for Practitioners and Teachers*, page 16.)

By the end of Phase Three children should:

- give the sound when shown all or most Phase Two and Phase Three graphemes;

- find all or most Phase Two and Phase Three graphemes, from a display, when given the sound;

- be able to blend and read CVC words (i.e. single-syllable words consisting of Phase Two and Phase Three graphemes);

- be able to segment and make a phonemically plausible attempt at spelling CVC words (i.e. single-syllable words consisting of Phase Two and Phase Three graphemes);

- be able to read the tricky words **he**, **she**, **we**, **me**, **be**, **was**, **my**, **you**, **her**, **they**, **all**, **are**;

- be able to spell the tricky words **the**, **to**, **I**, **no**, **go**;

- write each letter correctly when following a model.

Bank of suggested words, captions and sentences for use in Phase Three

The words in this section are made up from the letters taught for use in blending for reading and segmentation for spelling. These lists are not for working through slavishly but to be selected from as needed for an activity. (Words in italics are from the list of 100 high-frequency words.)

Words and sentences using sets 1–7 letters

Words using sets 1–6 GPCs

(+j)	(+v)	(+w)	(+x)
jam	van	*will*	mix
Jill	vat	win	fix
jet	vet	wag	box
jog	Vic	web	tax
Jack	Ravi	wig	six
Jen	Kevin	wax	taxi
jet-lag	visit	cobweb	vixen
jacket	velvet	wicked	exit

Words using sets 1–7 GPCs

(+y)	(+z/zz)	(+qu)
yap	zip	quiz
yes	Zak	quit
yet	buzz	quick
yell	jazz	quack
yum-yum	zigzag	liquid

Yes/no questions with words containing sets 1–6 GPCs

Is the sun wet?

Can wax get hot?

Has a fox got six legs?

Can a vet fix a jet?

Will a pen fit in a box?

Can men jog to get fit?

Has a pot of jam got a lid?

Can a taxi hop?

Can a van go up a hill?

Has a cat got a web?

Yes/no questions with words containing sets 1–7 GPCs

Can a duck quack?

Is a zebra a pet?

Can dogs yap?

Can a fox get wet?

Will a box fit in a van?

Can a rabbit yell at a man?

Can a hen peck?

Is a lemon red?

Is a robin as big as a jet?

Can a web buzz?

Sentences using words containing sets 1–7 GPCs and he, we and she

She will fill the bucket at the well.

If the dog has a bad leg, the vet can fix it.

Will Azam and Liz win the quiz? Yes!

He did up the zip on Zinat's jacket.

The fox and vixen had cubs in a den.

We can get the big bed into the van.

Sentences are offered here to give children practice in reading and understanding short texts which are fully decodable.

Words and sentences using Phase Three graphemes

Words using the four consonant digraphs

Each of these words contains the target grapheme but no other Phase Three graphemes. This means that the Phase Three graphemes can be taught in any order.

ch	sh	th	ng
chop	ship	*them*	ring
chin	shop	*then*	rang
chug	shed	*that*	hang
check	shell	*this*	song
such	fish	*with*	wing
chip	shock	moth	rung
chill	cash	thin	king
much	bash	thick	long
rich	hush	path (*north*)	sing
chicken	rush	bath (*north*)	ping-pong

Sentences with set 1–7 letters plus the four consonant digraphs and some tricky words

I am in such a rush to get to the shops.

A man is rich if he has lots of cash.

Natasha sang a song to me.

The van will chug up the long hill.

Sasha had a quick chat with Kath and me.

A moth can be fat, but its wings are thin.

The ship hit the rocks with a thud.

Lots of shops sell chicken as well as fish and chips.

Josh had a shock as he got a bash on the chin.

00281-2007BKT-EN

Words using the Phase Three vowel graphemes

ai	ee	igh	oa	oo	
wait	*see*	high	coat	*too*	*look*
Gail	feel	sigh	load	zoo	foot
hail	weep	light	goat	boot	cook
pain	feet	might	loaf	hoof	good
aim	jeep	night	road	zoom	book
sail	seem	right	soap	cool	took
main	meet	sight	oak	food	wood
tail	week	fight	toad	root	wool
rain	deep	tight	foal	moon	hook
bait	keep	tonight	boatman	rooftop	hood

ar	or	ur	ow	oi
bar	*for*	fur	*now*	oil
car	fork	burn	*down*	boil
bark	cord	urn	owl	coin
card	cork	burp	cow	coil
cart	sort	curl	how	join
hard	born	hurt	bow	soil
jar	worn	surf	pow!	toil
park	fort	turn	row	quoit
market	torn	turnip	town	poison
farmyard	cornet	curds	towel	tinfoil

ear	air	ure	er
ear	air	sure	hammer
dear	fair	lure	letter
fear	hair	assure	rocker
hear	lair	insure	ladder
gear	pair	pure	supper
near	cairn	cure	dinner
tear		secure	boxer
year		manure	better
rear		mature	summer
beard			banner

Words with a combination of two Phase Three graphemes

cheep	sheet	thing	thorn	teeth	coach
tooth	harsh	short	church	singer	shear
chair	waiter	arch	chain	faith	sheep
sharp	poach	shoal	shook	shark	march
torch	orchard	north	farmer	shorter	longer
looking	powder	lightning	porch	thicker	booth

Captions

tools in the shed

ships in port

boats on the river

fish and chips on a dish

a goat and a cow

sixteen trees

looking at books

the light of a torch

digging in the soil

goats in a farmyard

Sentences

Mark and Carl got wet in the rain.

Jill has fair hair but Jack has dark hair.

I can hear an owl hoot at night.

Bow down to the king and queen.

I can see a pair of boots on the mat.

The farmer gets up at six in the morning.

Jim has seven silver coins.

Nan is sitting in the rocking-chair.

Gurdeep had a chat with his dad.

It has been hot this year.

Sentences for the end of Phase Three

On the farm

I will soon visit my nan at her farm.

She will let me feed the hens and chickens.

They peck up corn in the farmyard.

She has goats and cows as well as hens.

She gets the hens into a shed at night
– foxes might get them.

In town

You and I can meet on the corner.

We can get the bus to the fish and chip shop.

Janaki and her sister may join us.

They can get fish and chips, too.

Then we can all run to the park.

In a wigwam

Kevin has a wigwam in the garden.

Alex, Jon and Jeevan visit him.

Kevin's dad cooks chicken for them on hot coals.

At the river

Max and Vikram sail a wooden boat.

Jeff chucks bits of bun in the river for the ducks.

Yasmin sits on a rock and looks for fish.

Having food in the wigwam is fun.
Then they sing songs.

Tanya and Yasha see an eel.
Shep the dog sits down in the mud and gets in a mess.

In the woods
Chip the dog runs to the woods.

He is looking for rabbits but sees a fox.

The fox sees him and rushes off to its den.

Chip dashes after it but cannot see it.

He feels sad and runs back to his kennel.

Sentences and substitute words for 'Sentence substitution'

See page 86.

Mark fed the cat	dog	hid	Gail	moon
The sheep are in the shed	bedroom	farmyard	cars	wait
You can hear a goat	toad	song	see	coin
They might meet in the town	market	summer	we	fish
The shop is on the corner	church	right	shark	boat
She has worn red shorts	boots	boats	seen	He
He sat down on the carpet	chair	fell	soil	weeds
She has had lots of good books	food	seen	hard	Joan
Join me in the pool	them	park	keep	coach
This is a good shop for chips	coats	year	coffee	bad

Yes/no questions suitable for the end of Phase Three

See page 97.

Is rain wet?

Can a boat sail?

Is all hair fair?

Is the moon far off?

Are fish and chips food?

Is it dark at night?

Is a thick book thin?

Can we get wool from sheep?

Will six cows fit in a car?

Can coins sing a song?

Will all shops sell nails?

Can a chicken sit on a chair?

Can a coach zoom into the air?

Are the teeth of sharks sharp?

Are fingers as long as arms?

Can a coat hang on a hook?

Can a hammer chop wood?

Will a ship sail on a road?

Can ducks see fish in rivers?

Can you hear bees buzzing now?

Letters and Sounds: Phase Four

Phase Four

(4–6 weeks)

Contents

Key

This icon indicates that the activity
can be viewed on the DVD.

Letters and Sounds: Principles and Practice of High Quality Phonics
Primary *National Strategy*

00281-2007BKT-EN

Summary

Children entering Phase Four will be able to represent each of 42 phonemes by a grapheme, and be able to blend phonemes to read CVC words and segment CVC words for spelling. They will have some experience in reading simple two-syllable words and captions. They will know letter names and be able to read and spell some tricky words.

The purpose of this phase is to consolidate children's knowledge of graphemes in reading and spelling words containing adjacent consonants and polysyllabic words.

The teaching materials in this phase provide a selection of suitable words containing adjacent consonants. These words are for using in the activities – practising blending for reading and segmenting for spelling. This is not a list to be worked through slavishly but to be selected from as needed for an activity.

It must always be remembered that phonics is the step up to word recognition. Automatic reading of all words – decodable and tricky – is the ultimate goal.

Suggested daily teaching in Phase Four

Sequence of teaching in a discrete phonics session

Introduction
Objectives and criteria for success

Revisit and review

Teach

Practise

Apply

Assess learning against criteria

Revisit and review

■ Practise previously learned graphemes

Teach

■ Teach blending and segmentation of adjacent consonants

■ Teach some tricky words

Practise

- Practise blending and reading words with adjacent consonants

- Practise segmentation and spelling words with adjacent consonants

Apply

- Read or write sentences using one or more high-frequency words and words containing adjacent consonants

Suggested timetable for Phase Four – discrete teaching

Week 1
- Practise recognition and recall of Phase Two and Three graphemes and reading and spelling CVC words
- Teach and practise reading CVCC words
- Teach and practise spelling CVCC words
- Teach reading the tricky words said, so
- Teach spelling the tricky words he, she, we, me, be
- Practise reading and spelling high-frequency words
- Practise reading sentences
- Practise writing sentences

Week 2
- Practise recognition and recall of Phase Two and Three graphemes and reading and spelling CVC words
- Teach and practise reading CCVC words
- Teach and practise spelling CCVC words
- Teach reading the tricky words have, like, some, come
- Teach spelling the tricky words was, you
- Practise reading and spelling high-frequency words
- Practise reading sentences
- Practise writing sentences

Week 3
- Practise recognition and recall of Phase Two and Three graphemes
- Practise reading words containing adjacent consonants
- Practise spelling words containing adjacent consonants
- Teach reading the tricky words were, there, little, one
- Teach spelling the tricky words they, all, are
- Practise reading and spelling high-frequency words
- Practise reading sentences
- Practise writing sentences

Week 4
- Practise recognition and recall of Phase Two and Three graphemes
- Practise reading words containing adjacent consonants
- Practise spelling words containing adjacent consonants
- Teach reading the tricky words do, when, out, what
- Teach spelling the tricky words my, her
- Practise reading and spelling high-frequency words
- Practise reading sentences
- Practise writing sentences

Letters and Sounds: Principles and Practice of High Quality Phonics
Primary *National Strategy*

00281-2007BKT-EN

Practising grapheme recognition for reading and recall for spelling

Grapheme recognition

Flashcards

Purpose

- To say as quickly as possible the correct sound when a grapheme is displayed

Resources

- Set of A4 size cards, one for each grapheme, or graphemes stacked on interactive whiteboard screen

Procedure

1. Hold up or slide into view the grapheme cards the children have learned, one at a time.

2. Ask the children to say, in chorus, the sound of the grapheme.

3. Increase the speed of presentation so that children learn to respond quickly.

Frieze

Resources

- Frieze of graphemes

- Pointing stick/hand

Procedure

1. Point to or remotely highlight graphemes, one at a time at random, and ask the children to tell you their sounds.

2. Gradually increase the speed.

3. You could ask a child to 'be teacher' as this gives you the opportunity to watch and assess the children as they respond.

Grapheme recall

Quickwrite graphemes

Resources

- Small whiteboards, pens and wipes, one per child or pair of children

Procedure

1. Say the sound of a grapheme (with the mnemonic and action if necessary) and ask the children to write it, saying the letter formation patter as they do so.

2. If the children are sharing a whiteboard both write, one after the other.

The children have already learned the formation of the letters that combine to form two-letter and three-letter graphemes but many may still need to say the mnemonic patter for the formation as they write. When referring to the individual letters in a grapheme, the children should be encouraged to use letter names (as the **t** in **th** does not have the sound of **t** as in top).

If you have taught the necessary handwriting joins, it may, at this point, be helpful to teach the easier digraphs as joined units (e.g. *ch*, *th*, *ai*, *ee*, *oa*, *oo*, *ow*, *oi* – see the reference to handwriting in *Notes of Guidance for Practitioners and Teachers*, page 15).

Teaching blending for reading CVCC and CCVC words

It must always be remembered that phonics is the step up to fluent word recognition. Automatic and effortless reading of all words – decodable and tricky – is the ultimate goal. By repeated sounding and blending of words, children get to know them, and once this happens, they should be encouraged to read them straight off in reading text, rather than continuing to sound and lend them aloud because they feel that this is what is required. They should continue, however, to use overt or silent phonics for those words which are unfamiliar.

CVCC words

Procedure

1. Display a CVC word on the whiteboard which can be extended by one consonant to become a CVCC word (e.g. tent).

2. Cover the final consonant and 'sound-talk' and blend the first three graphemes (e.g. **t-e-n** ten).

3. Ask the children to do the same.

4. Sound-talk the word again, **t-e-n** and as you say the **n**, reveal the final consonant and say -t tent.

5. Repeat 4 with the children joining in.

6. Repeat with other words such as bend, mend, hump, bent, damp.

CCVC words

Procedure

1. Display a CVC word on the whiteboard which can be preceded by one consonant to become a CCVC word (e.g. spot).

2. Cover the first letter and read the CVC word remaining (e.g. pot).

3. Reveal the whole word and point to the first letter and all say it together (e.g. **ssssss**) holding the sound as you point to the next consonant and slide them together and continue to sound-talk and blend the rest of the word.

4. Repeat with other words beginning with **s** (e.g. spin, speck, stop).

5. Move on to words where the initial letter sound cannot be sustained (e.g. trip, track, twin, clap, glad, gran, glass (north), grip).

Teaching segmenting for spelling CVCC and CCVC words

CVCC words

Resources

- Large four-phoneme frame drawn on a magnetic whiteboard
- List of words (visible only to the teacher) – see 'Bank of suggested words and sentences for use in Phase Four' on page 126
- Selection of magnetic letters (required to make the list of words) displayed on the whiteboard
- Small phoneme frames, each with the same selection of magnetic letters or six-grapheme fans, one per child or pair of children

Procedure

1. Say a word (e.g. **lost**) and then say it in sound-talk slightly accentuating the penultimate consonant **l-o-s-t**.

2. Repeat with another word.

3. Say another word (e.g. **dump**) and ask the children to tell their partners what it would be in sound-talk.

4. Make the word in the phoneme frame with the magnetic letters.

5. Say another word and ask the children to tell their partners what it would be in sound-talk.

6. Ask the children to tell you what letters to put in the phoneme frame.

7. Ask the children to make the word on their own phoneme frames or fans.

8. If all the children have frames or fans, ask them to check that they have the same answer as their partners. If the children are sharing, they ask their partners whether they agree.

9. Ask the children to hold up their frames or fans for you to see.

10. Repeat with other words.

This procedure can also be 'wrapped up' in a playful manner by 'helping a toy' to write words.

CVCC words

Follow the procedure for teaching segmenting CVCC words, accentuating the second consonant (e.g. **bring**).

Practising reading and spelling words with adjacent consonants

Large group – What's in the box?

Resources

- Set of word cards giving words with adjacent consonants: see 'Bank of suggested words and sentences for use in Phase Four', on page 126

- Set of objects or pictures corresponding to the word cards, hidden in a box

- Soft toy (optional)

Procedure

1. Display a word card.

2. Go through the letter recognition and blending process.

3. Ask the toy or a child to find the object in the box.

Variation

1. The children sit in two lines opposite one another.

2. Give the children in one line an object or picture and the children in the other line a word card.

3. The children with word cards read their words and the children with objects or pictures sound-talk the name of their object or picture to the child sitting next to them.

4. Ask the children to hold up their words and objects or pictures so the children sitting in the line opposite can see them.

5. Ask the children with word cards to stand up and go across to the child in the line opposite who has the corresponding object or picture.

6. All the children check that they have the right match.

Countdown

Resources

- List of Phase Four words

- Sand timer, stop clock or some other way of time-limiting the activity

Procedure

1. Display the list of words, one underneath the other.

2. Explain to the children that the object of this activity is to read as many words as possible before the sand timer or stop clock signals 'stop'.

3. Start the timer.

4. Call a child's name out and point to the first word.

5. Ask the child to sound-talk the letters and say the word.

6. Repeat with another child reading the next word until the time runs out.

7. Record the score.

The next time the game is played, the objective is to beat this score.

With less confident children this game could be played with all the children reading the words together.

Sentence substitution

Purpose

- To practise reading words in sentences

Resources

- A number of prepared sentences at the children's current level (see 'Bank of suggested words and sentences for use in Phase Four', page 128, for suggestions)

- List of alternative words for each sentence

Procedure

1. Write a sentence on the whiteboard (e.g. **The man burnt the toast**).

2. Ask the children to read the sentence with their partners and raise their hands when they have finished.

3. All read it together.

4. Rub out one word in the sentence and substitute a different word (e.g. **The man burnt the towel**).

5. Ask the children to read the sentence with their partners and raise their hands if they think it makes sense.

6. All read it together.

7. Continue substituting words – **The man burnt the towel**; **The girl burnt the towel**; **The girl burnt the milk**; **The girl brings the milk** – asking the children to read the new sentence to decide whether it still makes sense or is nonsense.

Small group with adult

The following activities can be played without an adult present but when they are completed the children seek out an adult to check their decisions.

Matching words and pictures

(Resources as for 'What's in the box?' above.)

Procedure

1. Lay out the word cards and pictures or objects on a table (involving the toy if you are using one)

2. Ask the children to match the words to the objects or pictures.

Buried treasure

Purpose

- To motivate children to read the words and so gain valuable reading practice

Resources

- About eight cards, shaped and coloured like gold coins with words and nonsense words on them, made up from letters the children have been learning (e.g. **skip**, **help**, **shelf**, **drep**, **plank**, **trunt**), in the sand tray

- Containers representing a treasure chest and a waste bin, or pictures of a treasure chest and a waste bin on large sheets of paper, placed flat on the table

Procedure

Ask the children to sort the coins into the treasure chest and the waste bin, putting the coins with proper words on them (e.g. **skip**) in the treasure chest and those with meaningless words (e.g. **drep**) in the waste bin.

Practising segmentation for spelling

Phoneme frame

Resources

- Large four-phoneme, five-phoneme or six-phoneme frame drawn on a magnetic whiteboard

- Selection of magnetic graphemes displayed on the whiteboard (the graphemes should be either custom-made as units or individual letters stuck together using sticky tape e.g. *ch*, *oa*)

- List of words (for use by the teacher)

- Small phoneme frames, each with a selection of magnetic letters or nine-grapheme fans, one per child or pair of children

Procedure

1. Say a CVCC word (e.g. **hump**) and then say it in sound-talk.

2. Say another CVCC word (e.g. **went**) and ask the children to tell their partners what it would be in sound-talk, showing a finger for each phoneme.

3. Demonstrate finding and placing the graphemes in the squares of the phoneme frame, sound-talk, **w-e-n-t** and then say **went**.

4. Say another CVCC word (e.g. **milk**) and ask the children to tell their partners what it would be in sound-talk.

5. Ask the children to tell you what to put in the first square in the phoneme frame, then in the next and so on.

6. Ask the children to make the word on their own phoneme frames or fans.

7. If all the children have frames or fans, ask them to check that they have the same answer as their partners. If the children are sharing, they ask their partners whether they agree.

8. Ask the children to hold up their frames or fans for you to see.

9. Repeat 4–8 with CCVC words and other words containing adjacent consonants.

This procedure can also be 'wrapped up' in a playful manner by 'helping a toy' to write words.

Quickwrite words

Resources

- Large four-phoneme, five-phoneme or six-phoneme frame drawn on a magnetic whiteboard

- List of words (for use by the teacher)

- Display of magnetic letters required for the words on the list

- Handheld phoneme frames on whiteboards, pens and wipes, one per child or pair of children

Procedure

1. Say a CCVC word and, holding up four fingers, sound-talk it, pointing to a finger at a time for each phoneme.

2. Ask the children to do the same and watch to check that they are correct.

3. Holding up the four fingers on one hand, write the letters of the word in the phoneme frame, consulting the letter display.

4. Ask the children to write the word in their phoneme frames.

5. Say another word and ask the children to sound-talk it to their partners using their fingers.

6. Ask them to sound-talk it in chorus for you to write it.

7. Repeat 5 and 6 but leave the last grapheme of the word for the children to write on their own.

8. Ask them to sound-talk (with fingers) and write more words that you say.

Teaching and practising high-frequency (common) words

There are 100 common words that recur frequently in much of the written material young children read and that they need when they write. Most of these are decodable, by sounding and blending, assuming the grapheme–phoneme correspondences are known. By the end of Phase Two 26 of the high-frequency words are decodable, a further 12 are decodable by the end of Phase Three and six more are decodable at Phase Four. These are: **went, it's, from, children, just** and **help**. Reading a group of these words each day, by applying grapheme–phoneme knowledge as it is acquired, will help children recognise them quickly. However, in order to read simple sentences it is necessary also to know some words that have unusual or untaught GPCs ('tricky' words) and these need to be learned (see *Notes of Guidance for Practitioners and Teachers*, page 15).

Learning to read tricky words

Resources

- Caption containing the tricky word to be learned

Procedure

1. Remind the children of some words with tricky bits that they already know (e.g **they, you, was**).

2. Read the caption, pointing to each word, and then point to the word to be learned and read it again.

3. Write the word on the whiteboard.

4. Sound-talk the word and repeat putting sound lines and buttons (as illustrated above) under each phoneme and blending them to read the word.

5. Discuss the tricky bit of the word where the letters do not correspond to the sounds the children know (e.g. in **so**, the last letter does not represent the same sound as the children know in **sock**).

6. Read the word a couple more times and refer to it regularly through the day so that by the end of the day the children can read the word straight away without sounding out.

Note: Although ending in the letter **e**, some, come and have are not split digraph words. It is easiest to suggest that the last phoneme is represented by a consonant and the letter **e**. It is not possible to show the phonemes represented by graphemes in the word one.

Practising reading high-frequency words

The six decodable and 14 tricky high-frequency words need lots of practice in the manner described below so that children will be able to read them 'automatically' as soon as possible.

Resources

- Between five and eight high-frequency words, including decodable and tricky words, written on individual cards

Procedure

1. Display a word card.

2. Point to each grapheme as the children sound-talk the graphemes (as far as is possible with tricky words) and read the word.

3. Say a sentence using the word, slightly emphasising the word.

4. Repeat 1–3 with each word card.

5. Display each word again, and repeat the procedure more quickly but without giving a sentence.

6. Repeat once more, asking the children to say the word without sounding it out.

Give the children a caption or sentence incorporating the high-frequency words to read at home.

Learning to spell and practising tricky words

he	she	we	me	be

was	my	you	her	they	all	are

Children should be able to read these words before being expected to learn to spell them.

Resources

- Whiteboards and pens, preferably one per child

Procedure

1. Write the word to be learned on the whiteboard and check that all the children can read it.

2. Say a sentence using the word.

3. Sound-talk the word raising a finger for each phoneme.

4. Ask the children to do the same.

5. Discuss the letters required for each phoneme, using letter names.

6. Ask the children to trace the shape of the letters on their raised fingers.

7. Rub the word off the whiteboard and ask the children to write the word on their whiteboards.

Practising reading and spelling two-syllable words

Reading two-syllable words

Resources

■ Short list of two-syllable words (for use by the teacher)

Procedure

1. Write a two-syllable word on the whiteboard making a slash between the two syllables (e.g. lunch/box).

2. Sound-talk the first syllable and blend it: **l-u-n-ch** lunch.

3. Sound-talk the second syllable and blend it: **b-o-x** box.

4. Say both syllables – lunchbox.

5. Repeat and ask the children to join in.

6. Repeat with another word.

Spelling two-syllable words

Resources

■ List of two-syllable words (for use by the teacher)

■ Whiteboards and magnetic letters or pens for each child

Procedure

1. Say a word (e.g. desktop), clap each syllable and ask the children to do the same.

2. Repeat with two or three more words.

3. Clap the first word again and tell the children that the first clap is on desk and the second is on top.

4. Ask the children for the sounds in desk and write the graphemes.

5. Repeat with the second syllable.

6. Read the completed word.

7. Repeat with another word.

8. Ask children to do the same on their whiteboards either by using magnetic letters or writing.

Reading sentences

Matching (with the teacher)

Resources

- Three pictures and a sentence corresponding to one of the pictures

Procedure

1. Display the pictures and the sentence (e.g. **It is fun to camp in a tent**).

2. Sound-talk (if necessary) and read the first word (e.g. **I-t It**).

3. After reading the second word, say both words (e.g. **i-s is** – It is).

4. Continue with the next word (e.g. **f-u-n fun** – It is fun).

5. Continue to the end of the sentence.

6. Ask the children which picture the sentence belongs to.

7. As children get more practice with high-frequency words, it should not be necessary to continue sound-talking them.

Matching (independent of the teacher)

Resources

- Set of pictures and corresponding sentences

Procedure

Ask the children to match the pictures and sentences.

Drawing

Resources

- Two sentences

Procedure

1. Display a sentence.

2. Ask the children to read it with their partners and draw a quick sketch.

3. Repeat with the next sentence.

'I can...' books

Purpose

- To practise reading

Resources

- Small zigzag book with 'I can skip' (jump, swim, clap, creep, swing, paint, etc.) sentences on one side of each page and a corresponding picture drawn by a child on the other

- Small four-page empty zigzag books made from half sheets of A4 paper (cut longwise)

- Action phrases (drink my milk, toast some cheese, punch a bag, hunt the slipper, brush my hair) on cards

- Paper copies of the action phrases, one per child

- Materials for writing, drawing and sticking

Procedure

1. Read the completed zigzag book to the children.

2. Show them the empty books for them to make their own.

3. Display the phrase cards, one a time, for the children to read.

4. Make available paper copies of the action phrases, the empty zigzag books, and writing, sticking and drawing materials for the children to make their own zigzag books.

Yes/no questions

Resources

- A number of prepared questions (see page 128 for suggestions) on card or an interactive whiteboard

- Cards with 'yes' on one side and 'no' on the other, one per pair of children

Procedure

1. Give pairs of children yes/no cards.

2. Display a yes/no question for the children to read.

3. Ask them to confer with their partners and decide whether the response is 'yes' or 'no'.

4. Ask the children to show their cards.

5. Invite a pair to read a question.

6. Repeat with another question.

Shared reading

When reading a shared text to the children occasionally locate words containing adjacent consonants and ask the children to read them.

Reading across the curriculum

Give the children simple written instructions. For instance, you could ask them to collect certain items from the outside area such as three sticks, some red string, etc. Children can read the labels on storage areas so they can collect the items they need and put them away.

Writing sentences

Writing sentences

Resources

- Picture including subjects with names that contain adjacent consonants and a sentence describing the picture

Procedure

1. Display and discuss the picture.

2. Ask the children to help you write a sentence for the picture (e.g. The clown did the best tricks).

3. Ask them to say the sentence all together a couple of times and then again to their partners.

4. Ask them to say it again all together two or three times.

5. Ask the children to tell you the first word.

6. Ask what letters are needed and write the word.

7. Ask about or point out the initial capital letter.

8. Remind the children that a space is needed between words and put a mark where the next word will start.

9. Ask the children to say the sentence again.

10. Ask for the next word and ask what letters are needed.

11. Repeat for each word.

12. Ask about or point out the full stop at the end of the sentence.

Shared writing

When writing in front of the children, take the occasional opportunity to ask them to help you spell words by telling you which letters to write.

Independent writing

When children are writing, for example in role-play areas, their letter knowledge along with their ability to segment will allow them to make a good attempt at writing many of the words they wish to use. Even though some of their spellings may be inaccurate, the experience gives them further practice in segmentation and, even more importantly, gives them experience in composition and helps them see themselves as writers (see the section on invented spelling in *Notes of Guidance for Practitioners and Teachers*, page 13). You will expect to see some of the tricky high-frequency words such as the, to, go, no, he, she, we and me spelled correctly during Phase Four.

Assessment

(See *Notes of Guidance for Practitioners and Teachers*, page 16.)

By the end of Phase Four children should:

- give the sound when shown any Phase Two and Phase Three grapheme;

- find any Phase Two and Phase Three grapheme, from a display, when given the sound;

- be able to blend and read words containing adjacent consonants;

- be able to segment and spell words containing adjacent consonants;

- be able to read the tricky words some, one, said, come, do, so, were, when, have, there, out, like, little, what;

- be able to spell the tricky words he, she, we, me, be, was, my, you, her, they, all, are;

- write each letter, usually correctly.

Bank of suggested words and sentences for use in Phase Four

The words in this section are made up from the letters taught for use in blending for reading and segmentation for spelling. These lists are not for working through slavishly but to be selected from as needed for an activity (words in italics are from the list of 100 high-frequency words).

CVCC words

Words using sets 1–7 letters			Words using Phase Three graphemes		Polysyllabic words	
went	best	fond	champ	shift	*children*	shampoo
it's	tilt	gust	chest	shelf	helpdesk	Chester
help	lift	hand	tenth	joint	sandpit	giftbox
just	lost	next	theft	boost	windmill	shelter
tent	tuft	milk	Welsh	thump	softest	lunchbox
belt	damp	golf	chimp	paint	pondweed	sandwich
hump	bust	jump	bench	roast	desktop	shelving
band	camp	fact	sixth	toast	helper	Manchester
dent	gift	melt	punch	beast	handstand	chimpanzee
felt	kept		chunk	think	melting	champion
gulp	tusk	(north)*	thank	burnt	seventh	thundering
lamp	limp	ask*				
wind	soft	fast*				
hump	pond	last*				
land	husk	daft*				
nest	cost	task*				
sink	bank					
link	bunk					
hunt						

*In the North of England, where the letter **a** is pronounced /a/, these are appropriate as Phase Four words.

CCV and CCVC words

Words using sets 1–7 letters		Words using Phase Three graphemes			
from	grip	green	flair	clear	speech
stop	glad	fresh	trail	train	smear
spot	twin	steep	cream	swing	thrill
frog	sniff	tree	clown	droop	
step	plum	spear	star	spoon	
plan	gran	smell	creep	float	Polysyllabic words
speck	swim	spoil	brown	smart	treetop
trip	clap	train	stair	groan	starlight
grab	drop	spoon	spoil	brush	floating
track	(north)*	sport	spark	growl	freshness
spin	glass*	thrush	bring	scoop	
flag	grass*	trash	crash	sport	
	brass*	start	bleed	frown	

CCVCC, CCCVC and CCCVCC words

Words using sets 1–7 letters			Words using Phase Three graphemes	Polysyllabic words
stand	crust	(north)*	crunch	driftwood
crisp	tramp	graft*	drench	twisting
trend	grunt	grant*	trench	printer
trust	crept	blast*	Grinch	
spend	drift	grasp*	shrink	
glint	slept	slant*	thrust	
twist	skunk			
brand	think		spring	
frost	thank		strap	
cramp	blink		string	
plump	drank		scrap	
stamp	blank		street	
blend	trunk		scrunch	
stunt				

Sentences

Fred and Brett spent a week in Spain.

I kept bumping into things in the dark.

Milk is good for children's teeth.

The clown did tricks with a chimpanzee.

The frog jumps in the pond and swims off.

I must not tramp on the flowers.

A crab crept into a crack in the rock.

A drip from the tap drops in the sink.

I can hear twigs snapping in the wind.

It is fun to camp in a tent.

Sentences and substitute words for 'Sentence substitution'

(See page 114)

The man burnt the toast.	towel	girl	milk	brings
The frog swam across the pool.	pond	flag	jumps	dog
Gran went to get fresh fish.	Stan	needed	meat	grill
Trisha took a book off the shelf.	grabs	desk	Krishnan	spoon
A clock stood on the wooden chest.	was	lamp	soft	cabinet
The train had to stop in the fog.	hand	wait	storm	truck
Fran took a scarf as a gift for Brad.	present	Vikram	sent	snail
I will travel to the Swiss Alps next week.	winter	punch	this	go
Fred has spent lots of cash this year.	Gretel	lost	lent	bricks
We had sandwiches for a snack.	plums	slugs	picnic	took

Yes/no questions

(See page 123)

Can a clock get cross?

Can crabs clap hands?

Are you fond of plums?

Did a shark ever jump up a tree?

Can frogs swim in ponds?

Is the moon green?

Can you bang on a big drum?

Have you ever slept in a tent?

Are all children good at sport?

Have you seen a trail left by a snail?

Are you afraid of thunderstorms?

Can a spoon grab a fork?

Do chimps come from Mars?

Can letters have stamps stuck on them?

Do trains run on tracks?

Will a truck go up steep stairs?

Do some dogs have black spots?

Are you glad when you have a pain?

Can we see the stars on a clear night?

Letters and Sounds: Principles and Practice of High Quality Phonics
Primary **National Strategy**

00281-2007BKT-EN

Letters and Sounds: **Phase Five**

Phase Five

(throughout Year 1)

Contents

Key

This icon indicates that the activity can be viewed on the DVD.

Letters and Sounds: Principles and Practice of High Quality Phonics
Primary **National Strategy**

00281-2007BKT-EN
© Crown copyright 2007

Summary

Children entering Phase Five are able to read and spell words containing adjacent consonants and some polysyllabic words. (See Appendix 3: Assessment.)

The purpose of this phase is for children to broaden their knowledge of graphemes and phonemes for use in reading and spelling. They will learn new graphemes and alternative pronunciations for these and graphemes they already know, where relevant. Some of the alternatives will already have been encountered in the high-frequency words that have been taught. Children become quicker at recognising graphemes of more than one letter in words and at blending the phonemes they represent. When spelling words they will learn to choose the appropriate graphemes to represent phonemes and begin to build word-specific knowledge of the spellings of words.

The teaching materials in this phase provide a selection of suitable words and sentences for use in teaching Phase Five. These words are for using in the activities – practising blending for reading and segmenting for spelling. These are not lists to be worked through slavishly but to be selected from as needed for an activity.

It must always be remembered that phonics is the step up to word recognition. Automatic reading of all words – decodable and tricky – is the ultimate goal.

Suggested daily teaching in Phase Five

Sequence of teaching in a discrete phonics session

Introduction
Objectives and criteria for success

Revisit and review

Teach

Practise

Apply

Assess learning against criteria

Revisit and review

■ Practise previously learned graphemes

■ Practise blending and segmentation

Teach

■ Teach new graphemes

■ Teach tricky words

Practise

■ Practise blending and reading words with the new GPC

■ Practise segmenting and spelling words with the new GPC

Apply

■ Read or write a sentence using one or more high-frequency words and words containing the new graphemes

Suggested timetable for Phase Five – discrete teaching

Weeks 1–4
- Practise recognition and recall of Phase Two, Three and Five graphemes as they are learned
- Teach new graphemes for reading (about four per week)
- Practise reading and spelling words with adjacent consonants and words with newly learned graphemes
- Learn new phoneme /**zh**/ in words such as **treasure**
- Teach reading the words **oh, their, people, Mr, Mrs, looked, called, asked**
- Teach spelling the words **said, so, have, like, some, come, were, there**
- Practise reading and spelling high-frequency words
- Practise reading and spelling polysyllabic words
- Practise reading sentences
- Practise writing sentences

Weeks 5–7
- Practise recognition and recall of graphemes and different pronunciations of graphemes as they are learned
- Teach alternative pronunciations of graphemes for reading (about four per week)
- Practise reading and spelling words with adjacent consonants and words with newly learned graphemes

- Teach reading the words **water**, **where**, **who**, **again**, **thought**, **through**, **work**, **mouse**, **many**, **laughed**, **because**, **different**, **any**, **eyes**, **friends**, **once**, **please**
- Teach spelling the words **little**, **one**, **do**, **when**, **what**, **out**
- Practise reading and spelling high-frequency words
- Practise reading and spelling polysyllabic words
- Practise reading sentences
- Practise writing sentences

Weeks 8–30

- Practise recognition and recall of graphemes and different pronunciations of graphemes as they are learned
- Teach alternative spellings of phonemes for spelling
- Practise reading and spelling words with adjacent consonants and words with newly learned graphemes
- Teach spelling the words **oh**, **their**, **people**, **Mr**, **Mrs**, **looked**, **called**, **asked**
- Practise reading and spelling high-frequency words
- Practise reading and spelling polysyllabic words
- Practise reading sentences
- Practise writing sentences

READING

It must always be remembered that phonics is the step up to fluent word recognition. Automatic and effortless reading of all words – decodable and tricky – is the ultimate goal. By repeated sounding and blending of words, children get to know them, and once this happens they should be encouraged to read them straight off in reading text, rather than continuing to sound and blend them aloud because they feel that this is what is required. They should continue, however, to use overt or silent phonics for words that are unfamiliar.

Teaching further graphemes for reading

New graphemes for reading

ay day	**oy** boy	**wh** when	**a-e** make
ou out	**ir** girl	**ph** photo	**e-e** these
ie tie	**ue** blue	**ew** new	**i-e** like
ea eat	**aw** saw	**oe** toe	**o-e** home
		au Paul	**u-e** rule

It is probably unnecessary to continue teaching mnemonics for new graphemes. As children build up their speed of blending and read more and more words automatically, many of them will assimilate new graphemes in the course of their reading. To ensure that all children know these graphemes, they should be quickly introduced through high-frequency words such as those suggested above.

Example session for split digraph i-e

Purpose

- To teach a split digraph through showing its relationship to a known grapheme

Resources

- Grapheme cards **t**, **m**, **p**, **n**, and **ie** × 2

- Scissors

- Reusable sticky pads

Procedure

1. Ask the children to sound-talk and show fingers for the word **tie** while a child makes it using the grapheme cards.

2. Ask the children what needs to be added to **tie** to make **time**.

3. Hold the **m** against the word **tie** thus making **tiem**, sound-talk it and explain that although there are graphemes for each phoneme this is not the correct spelling of **time**, as words like this are written slightly differently.

4. Cut the **ie** grapheme card between the **i** and the **e**, explaining that in this word we need to separate the two letters in the grapheme and tuck the final sound in between.

5. Stick the four letters onto the whiteboard and draw a line joining the **i** and the **e**.

6. Repeat with **pie** and make into **pine**.

7. Display or write on the whiteboard the high-frequency words that use the split digraph (e.g. **like**, **make**, **came**, **made**).

Teaching alternative pronunciations for graphemes

Known graphemes for reading: common alternative pronunciations

i fin, find	**ow** cow, blow	**y** yes, by, very
o hot, cold	**ie** tie, field	**ch** chin, school, chef
c cat, cent	**ea** eat, bread	**ou** out, shoulder, could, you
g got, giant	**er** farmer, her	
u but, put (*south*)	**a** hat, what	

Purpose

- To recognise that alternative pronunciations of some graphemes in some words need to be tried out to find the correct one

Resources

- Words on individual cards, half of the words illustrating one pronunciation of a grapheme and half illustrating the other (e.g. **milk, find, wild, skin, kind, lift, child**) – see 'Known graphemes for reading: alternative pronunciations' on page 152)

Procedure

1. Display a word where the vowel letter stands for the sound learned for it in Phase Two (e.g. **milk**) and ask the children to sound-talk and read it.

2. Display a word with the alternative pronunciation (e.g. **find**), sound-talk and read it using the incorrect pronunciation and therefore saying a nonsense word.

3. Discuss with the children which grapheme might have a different pronunciation (e.g. **find**).

4. Sound-talk the word again and read the word, this time correctly.

5. Display another word.

6. Ask the children to sound-talk it to their partners and decide the correct pronunciation.

7. Choose a pair of children and ask them to read the word.

8. Continue with more words.

Practising recognition of graphemes in reading words

Flashcards

Purpose

■ To say as quickly as possible the correct sound when a grapheme is displayed

Resources

■ Set of A4 size cards, one for each grapheme (or graphemes stacked on interactive whiteboard screen)

Procedure

1. Hold up or slide into view the grapheme cards the children have learned, one at a time.

2. Ask the children to say, in chorus, the sound of the grapheme.

3. Increase the speed of presentation so that children learn to respond quickly.

Frieze

Resources

■ Frieze of graphemes

■ Pointing stick/hand

Procedure

1. Point to or remotely highlight graphemes, one at a time at random, and ask the children to tell you their sounds.

2. Gradually increase the speed.

3. You could ask a child to 'be teacher' as this gives you the opportunity to watch and assess the children as they respond.

Quick copy

Purpose

■ To recognise two-letter and three-letter graphemes in words and not read them as individual letters

Resources

■ Words using some newly learned graphemes in which all graphemes of two or more letters are underlined (e.g. <u>pou</u>nd, l<u>igh</u>t, b<u>oy</u>, s<u>igh</u>, <u>ou</u>t, j<u>oy</u>)

■ Same words without the underlining (e.g. pound, light, boy, sigh, out, joy)

■ Magnetic whiteboards with all the appropriate graphemes to make the words, one per child

■ Extra letters to act as foils (e.g. if the grapheme **oy** is needed, provide separate letters **o** and **y** as well)

If custom-made graphemes are unavailable, attach letters together with sticky tape to make graphemes.

Procedure

1. Display a word in which the grapheme is underlined.

2. Ask the children to make the word as quickly as possible using their magnetic letters and saying the phonemes (e.g. **t-oy**) and then reading the word.

3. Check that, where appropriate, children are using joined letters, not the separate letters.

4. Repeat with each word with an underlined grapheme.

5. Repeat 1–4 with words without the underlined graphemes, being particularly vigilant that children identify the two-letter or three-letter graphemes in the words.

Countdown

Resources

■ List of Phase Five words

■ Sand timer, stop clock or some other way of time-limiting the activity

Procedure

1. Display the list of words, one underneath the other.

2. Explain to the children that the object of this activity is to read as many words as possible before the sand timer or stop clock signals 'stop'.

3. Start the timer.

4. Call a child's name out and point to the first word.

5. Ask the child to sound-talk the letters and say the word.

6. Repeat with another child reading the next word, until the time runs out.

7. Record the score.

The next time the game is played, the objective is to beat this score.

With less confident children this game could be played with all the children together reading the words.

Sentence substitution

Purpose

■ To practise reading words in sentences

Resources

■ A number of prepared sentences at the children's current level (see 'Word reading activities', on page 158, for suggestions)

■ List of alternative words for each sentence

Procedure

1. Write a sentence on the whiteboard (e.g. **Paul eats peas with his meat**).

2. Ask the children to read the sentence with their partners and raise their hands when they have finished.

3. All read it together.

4. Rub out one word in the sentence and substitute a different word (e.g. **Paul eats beans with his meat**).

5. Ask the children to read the sentence with their partners and raise their hands if they think it makes sense.

6. All read it together.

7. Continue substituting words – **Paul eats peas with his meat**; **Paul eats beans with his meat**; **Paul reads peas with his meat**; **Paul cooks peas with his meat** – asking the children to read the new sentence to decide whether it still makes sense or is nonsense.

Teaching and practising reading high-frequency (common) words

There are 100 common words that recur frequently in much of the written material young children read and that they need when they write. Most of these are decodable by sounding and blending, assuming the grapheme–phoneme correspondences are known. By the end of Phase Two, 26 of the high-frequency words are decodable; a further 12 are decodable by the end of Phase Three and six more at Phase Four. During Phase Five children learn many more graphemes so that more of these words become decodable. Some of them have already been taught as tricky words in earlier phases, leaving 16 to be decoded in Phase Five. These are **don't**, **day**, **here**, **old**, **house**, **made**, **saw**, **I'm**, **about**, **came**, **very**, **by**, **your**, **make**, **put** (*south*) and **time**. Reading a group of these words each day, by applying grapheme–phoneme knowledge as it is acquired, will help children recognise them quickly. However, in order to read simple sentences it is necessary also to know some words that have unusual or untaught GPCs ('tricky' words) and these need to be learned (see *Notes of Guidance* for *Practitioners and Teachers*, page 15, for an explanation).

Learning to read tricky words

oh	their	people	Mr*	Mrs*	looked	called	asked	would	should	could

*As shortened forms of words, **Mr** and **Mrs** cannot be taught in this way. You could write out **Mister** in full and show that the shortened version is the first and last letters, **Mr**. Then show how **Mrs** is a shortened version of **Mistress**.

The -**ed** morpheme at the end of **looked**, **called** and **asked** designates simple past tense and can be pronounced in a number of ways (/**t**/ in **looked** and **asked**, and /**d**/ in **called**).

Resources

- Caption or sentence containing the tricky word to be learned

Procedure

1. Remind the children of some of the other words with 'tricky bits' that they already know (e.g. **the**, **come**, **her**).

2. Read the caption pointing to each word, then point to the word to be learned and read it again.

3. Write the word on the whiteboard.

4. Sound-talk the word, and repeat putting sound lines and buttons (as illustrated on page 140) under each phoneme and blending them to read the word.

5. Colour and discuss the bit of the word that does not conform to standard GPC, i.e. the tricky bit (e.g. in **could**, the middle grapheme is not one of the usual spellings for the /**oo**/ sound).

6. Read the word a couple of times with the children joining in, and refer to it regularly during the day so that by the end of the day the children can read the word straight away without sounding out.

7. Ask the children do the same with their partners.

Practising reading high-frequency words

Both the decodable and tricky high-frequency words need lots of practice so that children will be able to read them 'automatically' as soon as possible.

Resources

■ Between five and eight high-frequency words, including decodable and tricky words, written on individual cards

Procedure

1. Display a word card.

2. Point to each grapheme as the children sound-talk the graphemes (as far as is possible with tricky words) and read the word.

3. Say a sentence using the word, slightly emphasising the word.

4. Repeat 1–3 with each word card.

5. Display each word again, and repeat the procedure more quickly but without giving a sentence.

6. Repeat once more, asking the children to say the word without sounding it out.

Give the children a caption or sentence incorporating the high-frequency words to read at home.

Practising reading two-syllable and three-syllable words

Resources

■ Short list of two-syllable and three-syllable words (for use by the teacher)

Procedure

1. Write a two-syllable word on the whiteboard making a slash between the two syllables (e.g. **thir/teen**).

2. Sound-talk the first syllable and blend it: **th-ir thir**.

3. Sound-talk the second syllable and blend it: **t-ee-n teen**.

4. Say both syllables: thirteen.

5. Repeat and ask the children to join in.

6. Repeat with another word.

Practising reading sentences

Yes/no questions

Resources

■ A number of prepared questions (see page 159 for suggestions) on card or an interactive whiteboard

■ Cards for each pair of children with 'yes' on one side and 'no' on the other, one per pair of children

Procedure

1. Give pairs of children yes/no cards.

2. Display a yes/no question for the children to read.

3. Ask them to confer with their partners and decide whether the response is 'yes' or 'no'.

4. Ask them to show their cards.

5. Sometimes invite a pair to read the question.

6. Repeat 2–5 with another question.

Variation

Choosing three right answers

Resources

■ A number of prepared questions or statements, three correct answers and one incorrect answer (see suggestions on page 159)

Procedure

As for 'Yes/no questions' except that children decide which of the four possible answers are correct.

Homographs

Purpose

■ To learn that when two words look the same the correct pronunciation can be worked out in the context of the sentence

Resources

■ Six sentences using homographs, for example:

  ○ **Wind** the bobbin up!

  ○ She will **read** it to her little brother.

  ○ The **wind** blew the leaves off the trees.

  ○ You have to **bow** when you meet the queen.

  ○ He **read** about the frightening monster.

  ○ Robin Hood used a **bow** and arrows.

Procedure

1. Display a sentence and read it using the incorrect pronunciation for the homograph.

2. Ask the children which word doesn't fit the sense of the sentence.

3. Try the alternative pronunciation and reread the sentence.

4. Display another sentence and ask the children to read it with their partners so it makes sense.

5. Ask a pair to read it aloud.

6. Continue with more sentences.

SPELLING

Teaching alternative spellings for phonemes

Alternative spellings for each phoneme

(See 'Bank of words and other materials/activities for use in Phase Five' on page 154.)

/c/	/ch/	/f/	/j/	/m/	/n/	/ng/	/r/	/s/	/sh/	/v/	/w/
k	tch	ph	g	mb	kn	n(k)	wr	c	ch	ve	wh
ck			dge		gn			sc	t(ion)		
qu									ss(ion, ure)		
x									s(ion, ure)		
ch									c(ion, ious, ial)		

/e/	/i/	/o/	/u/ (south)	/ai/	/ee/	/igh/	/oa/	/oo/	/oo/
ea	y	(w)a	o	ay	ea	y	ow	ew	u
	ey			a-e	e-e	ie	oe	ue	oul
				eigh	ie	i-e	o-e	ui	o (north)
				ey	y		o	ou	
				ei	ey				
					eo				

/ar/	/or/	/ur/	/ow/	/oi/	/ear/	/air/	/ure/	/er/
a (south)	aw	ir	ou	oy	ere	are	our	our
	au	er			eer	ear		e
	al	ear						u
	our							etc

New phoneme

/zh/
vision

Phoneme spotter

Purpose

■ To generate words containing the same target phoneme with a range of different spellings

■ To draw attention to the common ways to spell the target sound as a way of learning to spell the word

Resources

■ Phoneme spotter story (see examples on pages 160–165):

○ enlarged copy of the story for display

○ copies of the story, one per child or pair of children

■ coloured pencils or pens

Procedure

1. Display the enlarged version of the story.

2. Read the story to the children and ask them to listen out for the focus phoneme.

3. Remove the story from view and reread it, asking the children to put their thumbs up whenever they hear the focus phoneme.

4. Display the text again and read the title, pointing to each word.

5. Underline any word containing the focus phoneme.

6. Repeat with the first paragraph.

7. Ask the children to do the same on their copies.

8. Continue reading the story slowly while the children follow word by word, underlining each word that has the focus phoneme.

9. Ask the children to tell you which phonemes they spotted in the second paragraph and underline them on the enlarged copy.

10. Write on the whiteboard the first six underlined words in the story.

11. Ask the children to read the first word, sound-talk it and tell their partners what graphemes stand for the focus phoneme.

12. Ask a pair to tell you.

13. Repeat with the remaining words.

14. Notice the different graphemes that represent the focus phoneme.

15. Draw three columns on the whiteboard and write a different grapheme at the top of each column (e.g. **ai**, **ay**, **a-e**).

16. Write one word from the story under each grapheme (e.g. **rain**, **day**, **lane**).

17. Ask the children to draw three columns in their books or on paper and write the words from the story in the appropriate column.

Variation

Rhyming word generation

Procedure

1. Write a word on the whiteboard (e.g. **rain**).

2. Ask the children to suggest words that rhyme (e.g. **lane**, **Spain**) and write them on the whiteboard.

3. Write another word containing the same vowel phoneme (e.g. **date**) and ask the children to suggest words that rhyme and write them down.

4. Repeat with another word (e.g. **snake**).

5. Repeat with one more word, this time one that has the vowel phoneme at the end of it (e.g. **day**).

6. Pick any word and ask the children what grapheme represents the vowel phoneme.

7. Children discuss with their partners, write the grapheme on their whiteboards and hold them up.

8. Draw columns on the whiteboard and write the grapheme at the head of one column.

9. Ask the children to find a word with a different spelling of the phoneme.

10. Write the grapheme at the head of another column.

11. Repeat with another word until all alternative spellings for the vowel phonemes are written as column headers (e.g. **ai, ay, a-e, ea, aigh, eigh**).

12. Write one word under each grapheme (e.g. **rain**, **day**, **date**, **great**, **straight**, **eight**).

13. Ask the children to draw columns in their books or on paper and write the words from the whiteboard in the appropriate column.

14. Follow with 'Best bet' (below).

Best bet

Purpose

■ To develop children's knowledge of spelling choices

Resources

■ Lists of words generated from 'Phoneme spotter' (above) or a variation, under grapheme headers, for example as follows:

Common			Rare				
ay	**ai**	**a-e**	**ea**	**aigh**	**eigh**	**e-e**	**ey**
day	rain	lane	great	straight	eight	fete	they
play	wait	mate					
may	train	bake					
say	brain	snake					
tray	pain	late					
etc.	etc.	etc.					

■ Whiteboards and pens, one per child

Procedure

1. Display the lists of words.

2. Discuss which columns have most words in them and which the least. Point out that in English some spelling patterns are very rare but that some very common words (e.g. **they**) have rare spellings.

3. Ask the children if they can spot a pattern (e.g. the **ay** grapheme occurs at the end of words; the commonest spelling for the phoneme followed by **t** is **ate**; the commonest spelling for the phoneme followed by **k** is **ake**).

4. Ask the children to write a word not on display containing the same phoneme as some of the words listed (e.g. **hay**).

5. Where there are potentially two possible spellings ask the children to write which grapheme they think might be in a particular word and decide whether they think it is correct when they have looked at it written down.

6. The children then learn the correct spelling.

Learning to spell and practising high-frequency words

no	have	some	were	when
go	like	come	there	what
so	one	little	do	out

Children should be able to read these words before being expected to learn to spell them.

Resources

■ Whiteboards and pens, preferably one per child

Procedure

1. Write the word to be learned on the whiteboard and check that all the children can read it.

2. Say a sentence using the word.

3. Sound-talk the word raising a finger for each phoneme.

4. Ask the children to do the same.

5. Discuss the letters required for each phoneme, using letter names.

6. Ask the children to 'trace the shape of' the letters on their raised fingers.

7. Rub the word off the whiteboard and ask them to write the word on their whiteboards.

Note: Although ending in the letter **e**, **some**, **come** and **have** are not split digraph words. It is easiest to suggest that the last phoneme is represented by a consonant and the letter **e**. It is not possible to show the phonemes represented by graphemes in the word **one**.

Practising spelling two-syllable and three-syllable words

Resources

- List of words

- Whiteboards, pens and wipes, or pencil and paper for each child

Procedure

1. Say a word (e.g. **rescue**), clap each syllable and ask the children to do the same.

2. Repeat the clapping with two or three more words.

3. Clap the first word again and tell the children that the first clap is on **res** and the second is on **cue**.

4. Ask the children for the sounds in **res** and write them.

5. Repeat with the second syllable.

6. Read the completed word.

7. Repeat 3–6 with another word.

8. Continue with more words but the children write the words on their own whiteboards.

Practising writing sentences

> **Writing sentences**

Resources

- Sentence including words you wish to practise

Procedure

1. Ask the children to say the sentence all together a couple of times and then again to their partners.

2. Ask them to say it again all together two or three times.

3. Ask the children to tell you the first word.

4. Ask what letters are needed and write the word.

5. Ask about, or point out, the initial capital letter.

6. Remind the children that a space is needed between words and put a mark where the next word will start.

7. Ask the children to say the sentence again.

8. Ask for the next word and ask what letters are needed.

9. Repeat for each word.

10. Ask about or point out the full stop at the end of the sentence.

Independent writing

When children are writing, for example in role-play areas, their letter knowledge along with their ability to segment will allow them to make a good attempt at writing many of the words they wish to use. Even though some of their spellings may be partially inaccurate, the experience gives them further practice in segmentation and, even more importantly, gives them experience in composition and makes them see themselves as writers. Children should be able to spell most of the 100 high-frequency words accurately during the course of Phase Five.

Assessment

(See 'Notes of Guidance for Practitioners and Teachers', page 16.)

By the end of Phase Five children should:

■ give the sound when shown any grapheme that has been taught;

■ for any given sound, write the common graphemes;

■ apply phonic knowledge and skill as the prime approach to reading and spelling unfamiliar words that are not completely decodable;

■ read and spell phonically decodable two-syllable and three-syllable words;

■ read automatically all the words in the list of 100 high-frequency words;

■ accurately spell most of the words in the list of 100 high-frequency words;

■ form each letter correctly.

Bank of words and other materials for use in Phase Five activities

Some new graphemes for reading

Words in italics are high-frequency words.

ay	ou	ie	ea	oy	ir	ue	ue
day	*out*	pie	sea	boy	girl	clue	cue
play	*about*	lie	seat	toy	sir	blue	due
may	cloud	tie	bead	joy	bird	glue	hue
say	scout	die	read	oyster	shirt	true	venue
stray	found	cried	meat	Roy	skirt	Sue	value
clay	proud	tried	treat	destroy	birth	Prue	pursue
spray	sprout	spied	heap	Floyd	third	rue	queue
tray	sound	fried	least	enjoy	first	flue	statue
crayon	loudest	replied	steamy	royal	thirteen	issue	rescue
delay	mountain	denied	repeat	annoying	thirsty	tissue	argue

aw	wh	wh
saw	*when*	*who*
paw	*what*	*whose*
raw	*which*	*whole*
claw	*where*	*whom*
jaw	*why*	*whoever*
lawn	whistle	
yawn	whenever	
law	wheel	
shawl	whisper	
drawer	white	

ph	ew	ew	oe	au	ey
Philip	blew	stew	toe	Paul	money
Philippa	chew	few	hoe	haul	honey
phonics	grew	new	doe	daub	donkey
sphinx	drew	dew	foe	launch	cockney
Christopher	screw	pew	woe	haunted	jockey
dolphin	crew	knew	Joe	Saul	turkey
prophet	brew	mildew	goes	August	chimney
phantom	flew	nephew	tomatoes	jaunty	valley
elephant	threw	renew	potatoes	author	trolley
alphabet	Andrew	Matthew	heroes	automatic	monkey

a-e	e-e	i-e	o-e	u-e
came	these	like	bone	June
made	Pete	time	pole	flute
make	Eve	pine	home	prune
take	Steve	ripe	alone	rude
game	even	shine	those	use
race	theme	slide	stone	rule
same	gene	prize	woke	
snake	scene	nice	note	
amaze	complete	invite	explode	
escape	extreme	inside	envelope	

Known graphemes for reading: alternative pronunciations

a		e	i	o	u	
hat		bed	tin	hot	but	
acorn	fast**	he	mind	no	unit	put**
bacon	path**	me	find	so	union	pull**
apron	pass**	she	wild	go	unicorn	push**
angel	father**	we	pint	old	music	full**
apricot	bath**	be	blind	don't	tuba	bush**
bagel	last**	the*	child	gold	future	bull**
station	grass**	recent	kind	cold	human	cushion**
nation	after**	frequent	grind	told	stupid	awful**
Amy	branch**	region	behind	both	duty	playful**
lady	afternoon**	decent	remind	hold	humour	pudding**

* before a vowel

** In the North of England the grapheme **a** is pronounced the same in **hat**, **fast**, etc. The grapheme **u** is pronounced the same in **but**, **put**, etc. Alternative pronunciations for each of these graphemes apply in the South of England only.

ow

down	low
	low
	grow
	snow
	glow
	bowl
	tow
	show
	slow
	window
	rowing-boat

ie

sea	pie	chief
		chief
		brief
		field
		shield
		priest
		yield
		shriek
		thief
		relief
		belief

ea

	head
	head
	dead
	deaf
	ready
	bread
	heaven
	feather
	pleasant
	instead
	breakfast

er

farmer	her
	her
	fern
	stern
	Gerda
	herbs
	jerky
	perky
	Bernard
	servant
	permanent

ou

out	you	could	mould
	you	could	mould
	soup	would	shoulder
	group	should	boulder

ch

chin	school	chef
	school	chef
	Christmas	Charlene
	chemist	Chandry
	chord	Charlotte
	chorus	machine
	Chris	brochure
	chronic	chalet
	chemical	
	headache	
	technical	

c

cat	cell	got
	cell	got
	central	
	acid	
	cycle	
	icy	
	cent	
	Cynthia	
	success	
	December	
	accent	

g

got	gent
	gent
	gym
	gem
	Gill
	gentle
	ginger
	Egypt
	magic
	danger
	energy

y

yes	by	gym	very
	by	gym	very
	my	crystal	happy
	try	mystery	funny
	why	crystal	carry
	dry	pyramid	hairy
	fry	Egypt	smelly
	sky	bicycle	penny
	spy	Lynne	crunchy
	fry	cygnet	lolly
	reply	rhythm	merrily

ey

money	they
	grey
	obey
	prey
	survey

Alternative spellings for each phoneme

/ch/	/j/	/m/	/n/	/n/	/r/
picture	fudge	lamb	gnat	knit	wrap
adventure	hedge	limb	gnaw	knob	wren
creature	bridge	comb	gnash	knot	wrong
future	ledge	climb	gnome	knee	wrench
nature	nudge	crumb	sign	knock	write
capture	badge	dumb	design	knife	wrote
feature	lodge	thumb	resign	know	wreck
puncture	podgy	numb		knew	wry
signature	badger	plumbing		knight	written
mixture	dodging	bomber		knuckle	wretched

/s/	/s/	/z/	/u/*	/i/	/i/	/ear/	/ear/
listen	house	please	some	happy	donkey	here	beer
whistle	mouse	tease	come	sunny	valley	mere	deer
bristle	grease	ease	done	mummy	monkey	severe	jeer
glisten	cease	rouse	none	daddy	chimney	interfere	cheer
Christmas	crease	browse	son	only	trolley	Windermere	peer
rustle	horse	cheese	nothing	gym	pulley	adhere	sneer
jostle	gorse	noise	month	crystal	Lesley		sheer
bustle	purse	pause	mother	mystery			veer
castle	grouse	blouse	worry	sympathy			career
wrestling	loose	because	brother	pyramid			steering

* The phoneme /u/ is not generally used in North of England accents.

/ar/		/air/			/or/		
father	half	there	pear	bare	all	four	caught
lather	calf	where	bear	care	always	pour	taught
rather	almond	nowhere	wear	dare	talk	your	naughty
pass*	calm	somewhere	tear	fare	walk	court	haughty
path*	qualm	everywhere	swear	hare	wall	fourth	daughter
bath*	lip balm			mare	fall	Seymour	Vaughan
last*	palm tree			square	ball	tour*	
grass*				scare	hall	mourn*	
afternoon*				stare	calling	fourteen	
branching*				share	beanstalk	tournament	

* The classification of these words is very dependent on accent.

/ur/		/oo/	
learn	word	*could*	*put*
earn	work	would	pull
earth	world	should	push
pearl	worm		full
early	worth		bush
search	worse		bull
heard	worship		cushion
earnest	worthy		pudding
rehearsal	worst		playful

/ai/		/ee/					/igh/		
day	*came*	sea	these	happy	chief	key	pie	by	like
play	*made*	seat	Pete	sunny	brief	donkey	lie	my	time
may	*make*	bead	Eve	mummy	field	valley	tie	try	pine
say	take	read	Steve	daddy	shield	monkey	cried	why	ripe
stray	game	meat	even	only	priest	chimney	tried	dry	shine
clay	race	treat	theme	funny	yield	trolley	spied	fry	slide
spray	same	heap	complete	sadly	shriek	pulley	fried	sky	prize
tray	snake	least	Marlene	penny	thief	Lesley	replied	spy	nice
crayon	amaze	steamy	gene	heavy	relief	money	applied	deny	decide
delay	escape	repeat	extreme	quickly	belief	honey	denied	reply	polite

/oa/			/(y) oo/			/oo/		
low	toe	bone	cue	tune	stew	clue	June	blew
grow	hoe	pole	due	cube	few	blue	flute	chew
snow	doe	home	hue	tube	new	glue	prune	grew
glow	foe	woke	venue	use	dew	true	rude	drew
bowl	woe	those	value	cute	pew	Sue	fluke	screw
tow	Joe	stone	pursue	duke	knew	Prue	brute	crew
show	goes	woke	queue	huge	mildew	rue	spruce	brew
slow	Glencoe	note	statue	mule	nephew	flue	plume	flew
window	heroes	phone	rescue	amuse	renew	issue	rule	threw
rowing boat	echoes	alone	argue	computer	Matthew	tissue	conclude	Andrew

/sh/			
special	station	sure	chef
official	patience	sugar	Charlotte
social	caption	passion	Charlene
artificial	mention	session	Michelle
facial	position	mission	Chandry

New phoneme

treasure
television
vision
pleasure
leisure
beige
visual
measure
usual
casual

Sentences and substitute words for 'sentence substitution'

(See page 139.)

New graphemes for reading

Paul eats peas with his meat.	beans	reads	cooks	Phil
Kay must pay for her new bike.	toes	Jean	wait	toy
We can bake a pie today.	they	yesterday	cake	make
The boys shout as they play outside.	sleep	girls	run	sing
They saw that the dog had hurt its paw.	found	she	tail	stone
Children like the seaside.	dentist	beach	enjoy	zoo
Loud sounds can be annoying.	noises	singing	frightening	mountains
Mum gave us a few grapes as a treat.	sold	made	punishment	Dad
The girl came home on the train.	bird	bus	went	boy
You can tie things up with string.	rope	we	glue	ribbon

More reading practice with old and new GPCs

Chris found his wallet in the drawer.	shirt	socks	Charlie	saw
Soup is a healthy kind of food.	wealthy	fish	sport	sort
Grown-ups teach us at school.	help	goblins	teachers	home
Snow and rain are part of our winter weather.	summer	wind	cold	frost
You can see clowns at a circus.	elephants	watch	market	acrobats
We could fly to Africa in a plane.	ship	you	might	go
The thief was kept in prison.	robber	put	oyster	jail
We can make models from card.	tea	clay	children	wood
Cows and sheep may graze in a meadow.	goats	field	stay	sail
The puppy was very playful.	kitten	cute	kitchen	hungry

Questions for Yes/no questions

(See page 142)

Could you carry an elephant on your head?

Would you like to wave a magic wand?

Would you crawl into a thorn bush?

Have you ever seen a live crocodile?

Are you ready for school by nine in the morning?

Could a cactus grow in Antarctica?

Would you scream if you saw a snake?

Can magpies perch on clouds in the sky?

Would you put ice-cream in the freezer?

Has a cat got sharp claws?

Do you go to school in the holidays?

Is December a summer month?

Could you fly to Mars on a bike?

Has a space-ship ever been to the moon?

Could you make up a story about a giant?

Examples for 'Choosing three right answers'

(See page 143)

Which of these are days of the week?	Sunday	Thursday	Tuesday	September
Which are names for girls?	Heather	Hayley	Sanjay	Philippa
Which of these are numbers?	blue	five	nine	thirteen
Which of these can we read?	news	comics	see-saws	books
Traffic lights can be	green	white	yellow	red
Which of these are parts of the body?	cry	head	elbow	chin
A chef can cook food by	boiling	grilling	flying	frying
What can you put on bread?	jam	butter	cheese	coffee
Which of these can grow in a garden?	ferns	snow	herbs	bushes
Which of these could you hold in your hand?	a giant	a jewel	a feather	a penny

Phoneme spotter stories

A Real Treat!

Tom was very happy. It was the weekend and he was off to the beach with Mum and Dad, his puppy and baby Pete.

"Help me pack the green bag," said Mum. "We need sun cream and lots to eat."

Tom got into his seat in the back of the car and the puppy got on his knee. Pete held his toy sheep. Off they went. Beep! Beep!

At the end of the street there was a big truck. It had lost a wheel. "Oh, no," said Tom. "We'll be here for a week!"

Dad went to speak to the driver to see if he could help. They put the wheel back on. Then Dad said, "I must hurry. We need to get to the beach."

At last they got to the sea. Tom and Pete had an ice-cream. Mum and Dad had a cup of tea. The puppy went to sleep under a tree.

A Right Mess

The twins' bedroom was a right mess! Mum had tried everything. Being cross! Being kind! But it just did not help. The twins still did not tidy their room.

Then Mum had an idea. "I think I'll write a list of things the twins must pick up, and then we can play a game of hide and seek. The twins must find the things and put them in a box. Their room will be tidy!"

This is the list Mum had:

A crisp bag

A white sock

A tie with a stripe

A cap

A plastic knife

A bright red kite

"We like this game of hide and seek," said the twins. In no time at all the room was quite tidy and Mum was happy.

Then the twins had an idea. "Mum, we'd like to fly this kite on the green."

"All right," said Mum, "but you must hold the string tight."

On the green there was a light breeze and the kite went up, up, up, high in the sky. Then suddenly it came down, down, down...

CRASH! It fell into the duck pond!

The kite was fine, but Mum said, "I think it's time for tea. Let's go home."

Luke and Ruth

It was Saturday and Luke went to play at Ruth's house. Ruth and her mum lived in the house next to Luke's house.

"Let's go outside," said Ruth as she put her blue boots on. "Do you need boots too?"

"I do. I'll nip home and take my new shoes off." said Luke, "I'll be back soon."

Luke came back and the two of them began to dig. "Can I use the spade?" said Luke.

"Yes. Can you help me move this big root?" said Ruth. "Then we can sow the seeds." Luke and Ruth soon had the seeds in the ground and they made the earth smooth on top. "Now we will wait until they grow," they said.

Two weeks later, Ruth ran to Luke's house. "Quick! The seeds are growing." Luke ran round to see if it was true. It was. In the next few weeks they grew and grew and, in June, they had blue flowers.

"Our blue flowers are super," said Luke.

"The best," said Ruth.

The Old Pony

Joe, the old pony, was in his field. He was so old and slow that nobody rode him anymore. The wind was blowing. He felt cold and lonely.

Just then, Jazz and Hal rode by on their bikes. They were going home for tea. They felt so sorry for old Joe that they stopped to stroke him.

At tea time they told Dad about Joe.

"Don't worry," said Dad. "I know I can help him."

After tea, Dad went to the shed and got an old green coat and a thin rope. Jazz and Hal got the end of a loaf of bread.

"Let's go," said Dad.

Dad and Jazz and Hal went back to Joe's field.

"Hello, old fellow," said Dad. Quickly, he put the old coat over Joe's back and tied it on with rope. In no time at all, Joe was as warm as toast!

Jazz and Hal gave Joe some of the loaf to eat. Old Joe was happy at last.

The School Sale

It was the day of the school sale. Mum could not go as she had a pain in her knee, so Gran said she would take Kate and Wayne. They could not wait!

At the school gate, Gran paid 20p to get in. She did not have to pay for Kate and Wayne – it was free for children!

As soon as they were through the gate, Gran gave Wayne and Kate £1 each to spend, and told them not to go too far away.

The sun was shining. "It's as hot as Spain!" said Gran. "I think I need a cup of tea."

At the tea stall, a lady put Gran's tea on a tray, and Gran went to find a place to sit in the shade.

Meanwhile, Kate and Wayne went round the stalls. Kate had her face painted like a rainbow and had a go on the "Name a Teddy" stall. Wayne bought a game of chess and a piece of chocolate cake for Mum. They both had a go on the "Pin the tail on the donkey". It was quite safe – the donkey was only made of paper!

When the sale was nearly over, Kate and Wayne went back and found Gran fast asleep under the tree. "What a shame," said Kate, "she's missed all the fun!"

Could I?

Mr and Mrs Hood had a house by the sea. Mr Hood was a fisherman. When he was away on a fishing trip, Mrs Hood would get very lonely and sad.

"I need a job," she said to herself. "I like to look at books, I could sell books in the bookshop."

She went to the bookshop but the people there said "No."

"This is no good," Mrs Hood said to herself, "I should stop and think." Mrs Hood sat and had a good long think and then she said, "I like to cook. I could run a cake shop."

She began to cook and in next to no time her house was full of the smell of cakes and pies. She put a poster up on the gate that said, "Home-made cakes and pies". She sold everything she had made.

She told Mr Hood about it when he came home. "I would like to try a cake," he said, "I'm hungry."

"I'm sorry," Mrs Hood said, "I sold out."

Letters and Sounds: **Phase Six**

Phase Six

(throughout Year 2)

Contents

Key

This icon indicates that the activity
can be viewed on the DVD.

Letters and Sounds: Principles and Practice of High Quality Phonics
Primary *National Strategy*

00281-2007BKT-EN

Summary

By the beginning of Phase Six, children should know most of the common grapheme–phoneme correspondences (GPCs). They should be able to read hundreds of words, doing this in three ways:

- reading the words automatically if they are very familiar;

- decoding them quickly and silently because their sounding and blending routine is now well established;

- decoding them aloud.

Children's spelling should be phonemically accurate, although it may still be a little unconventional at times. Spelling usually lags behind reading, as it is harder. (See Appendix 3: Assessment.)

During this phase, children become fluent readers and increasingly accurate spellers.

READING

At this stage many children will be reading longer and less familiar texts independently and with increasing fluency. The shift from learning to read to reading to learn takes place and children read for information and for pleasure.

Children need to learn some of the rarer GPCs (see *Notes of Guidance for Practitioners and Teachers*, Appendix 2, page 19,) and be able to use them accurately in their reading.

A few children may be less fluent and confident, often because their recognition of graphemes consisting of two or more letters is not automatic enough. Such children may still try to use phonics by sounding out each letter individually and then attempting to blend these sounds (for instance /**c**/-/**h**/-/**a**/-/**r**/-/**g**/-/**e**/ instead of /**ch**/-/**ar**/-/**ge**/). This is all too often misunderstood by teachers as an overuse of phonics rather than misuse, and results in teachers suggesting to children that they use alternative strategies to read unfamiliar words. Instead the solution is greater familiarity with graphemes of two or more letters. The necessity for complete familiarity with these graphemes cannot be overstated. The work on spelling, which continues throughout this phase and beyond, will help children to understand more about the structure of words and consolidate their knowledge of GPCs. For example, children who are not yet reliably recognising digraphs and are still reading them as individual letters will get extra reinforcement when they learn to spell words containing the digraphs such as **road, leaf, town, cloud, shop**.

As children find that they can decode words quickly and independently, they will read more and more so that the number of words they can read automatically builds up. There is a list of the 300 high-frequency words in Appendix 1 on pages 193–195. Increasing the pace of reading is an important objective. Children should be encouraged to read aloud as well as silently for themselves.

Knowing where to place the stress in polysyllabic words can be problematic. If the child has achieved a phonemic approximation of the word, particularly by giving all vowels their full value, the context of the sentence will often provide a sensible resolution; the child should then recheck this against the letters. Working through the word in this way will make it easier for it to be read more automatically in future.

In Phase Six, many children will be able to read texts of several hundred words fluently at their first attempt. Those children who are less fluent may benefit from rereading shorter texts several times, not in order to memorise the texts, but to become more familiar with at least some of the words that cause them to stumble, and to begin to experience what fluent reading feels like.

To become successful readers, children must understand what they read. They need to learn a range of comprehension strategies and should be encouraged to reflect upon their own understanding and learning. Such an approach, which starts at the earliest stages, gathers momentum as children develop their fluency. Children need to be taught to go beyond literal interpretation and recall, to explore the greater complexities of texts through inference and deduction. Over time they need to develop self-regulated comprehension strategies:

- activating prior knowledge;

- clarifying meanings – with a focus on vocabulary work;

- generating questions, interrogating the text;

- constructing mental images during reading;

- summarising.

Many of the texts children read at this stage will be story books, through which they will be developing an understanding of the author's ideas, plot development and characterisation. It is important that children are also provided with opportunities to read a range of non-fiction texts, which require a different set of strategies. The use of a contents page, index and glossary makes additional demands on young readers as they search for relevant information. In reading simple poems, children need to adapt to and explore the effects of poetic language, continuing to develop their understanding of rhythm, rhyme and alliteration.

From an early stage, children need to be encouraged to read with phrasing and fluency, and to take account of punctuation to aid meaning. Much of the reading now will be silent and children will be gaining reading stamina as they attempt longer texts.

In addition, as children read with growing independence, they will engage with and respond to texts; they will choose and justify their choice of texts and will begin to critically evaluate them.

It is important throughout that children continue to have opportunities to listen to experienced readers reading aloud and that they develop a love of reading.

SPELLING

Teaching spelling

> ### Introducing and teaching the past tense
>
> The past tense dealt with in this section is simple past tense, e.g. **I looked**, not continuous past tense, e.g. **I was looking**.
>
> Before you teach children to spell the past tense forms of verbs, it is important that they gain an understanding of the meaning of 'tense'. Since many common verbs have irregular past tenses (e.g. **go – went**, **come – came**, **say – said**) it is often easier to teach the *concept* of past tense separately from the *spelling* of past tense forms. Short oral games can be used for this purpose.
>
> For example, a puppet could say *Today I am eating an egg – what did I eat yesterday?* The response could be *Yesterday you ate a sandwich*, *Yesterday you ate some jam*. The puppet could say *Today I am jumping on the bed. Where did I jump yesterday?* and the response could be *Yesterday you jumped in the water*, etc. These games can be fitted into odd moments now and then; several children could respond in turn, and the games would also serve as memory training (don't repeat what's already been suggested).
>
> ### Using familiar texts
>
> *Procedure*
>
> Use a current class text as the basis for discussion about tense.
>
> 1. Find extracts of past tense narrative and ask children to describe what is happening in the present tense. For example, use extracts from *Funnybones* (by Alan Alhberg and Janet Alhberg, published by Puffin Books) such as where the skeletons leave the cellar, climb the stairs and walk to the park.
>
> 2. Let the children compare the two versions. Discuss how they are different both in meaning and language.
>
> 3. Use the words **yesterday** and **today** to reinforce the different meanings.
>
> 4. Find bits of present tense dialogue in the text and ask children to retell it as past tense narrative.

Investigating and learning how to add suffixes

Phoneme frame

Purpose

■ To reinforce understanding and application of the -**ed** suffix for the past tense

Prerequisite

■ The children must have an understanding of the grammar of the past tense and experience of segmenting words into phonemes

Resources

For whole-class work

■ Set of five-box and six-box phoneme frames drawn on the whiteboard

■ Set of five-box and six-box phoneme frames, on laminated card so they can be reused, one per pair of children

■ Word cards placed in a bag (e.g. **rounded**, **helped**, **turned**, **begged**, **hissed**, **wanted**, **sorted**, **hummed**, **waded**, **washed**, **hated**, **greased**, **lived**, **robbed**, **rocked**, **laughed**, **called**, **roasted**)

Procedure

1. Pick a word card from the bag and read it out without showing the children.

2. Working with a partner, the children say the word to themselves then segment and count the phonemes. They decide which phoneme frame to use and try writing it with one phoneme in each box.

3. Say *Show me* as the signal for the children to hold up their frames.

4. Demonstrate how to spell the word correctly using a frame on the whiteboard and ask the pairs of children to check their own spellings.

5. Repeat for about six words and look at the words that have been written. What spelling pattern do they all have? Emphasise that even when the final phoneme sounds different (e.g. **jumped**), the spelling pattern is still the same. Challenge the children to explain why this is (past tense of verbs). Look closely at the phoneme frames. Sometimes the -**ed** ending is two phonemes (e.g. **wanted**) and sometimes only one (e.g. **grasped**).

Word sort

Purpose

■ To categorise words according to their spelling pattern

Use this activity to investigate:

■ the rules for adding -**ing**, -**ed**, -**er**, -**est**, -**ful**, -**ly** and -**y**, plurals (see pages 189–190)

■ how to differentiate spelling patterns (e.g. different representations of the same phoneme; the 'w special' – see page 187).

Resources

For whole-class work

■ Set of word cards exemplifying the spelling patterns you are investigating (see 'Practice examples', on page 191, for suggestions)

■ Reusable sticky pads

For independent work

■ Different set of word cards, with words tailored to the children's ability, one per pair or group of three children

Procedure

Whole-class work

1. Select a word, read it out and attach it to the top of the whiteboard. Underline the part of the word that you are looking at and explain what you are investigating (e.g. how the vowel phoneme is spelt; how the base word has changed).

2. Ask the children to identify other words that follow the same pattern. Challenge them to explain their suggestion and then move the words into the column.

3. When all the words have been identified, start a new column and ask the children to explain what is different about this spelling pattern.

4. If they suggest a word that does not fit the pattern, start a new column and challenge them to find other words that would go with it.

5. When the words have been sorted, ask the children to suggest spelling rules based on what they can see. Note their suggestions so that they can refer to them in independent work.

Independent work

1. Provide more word cards for the children to sort, working in pairs or groups of three.

2. The children use the same categories as before and take it in turns to place a word in one of the columns. The other group members must agree.

3. Words that they cannot place can go into a 'problem' pile.

4. The group compose a label for each column that explains what the words have in common.

Plenary

1. Look back at the rules that were suggested earlier and ask the children whether they were able to apply them when they sorted their own words.

2. Look at the 'problem' words and help the children to categorise them. Talk about exceptions to the general rules and ways to remember these spellings.

Add race

Purpose

■ To practise adding -**ing**

Use this activity to revisit the rules for: adding -**ing**, adding -**ed**, adding -**s** and adding suffixes -**er**, -**est**, -**ful**, -**ly** and -**y**. (see pages 189–190)

(The activity is described as if the focus were adding -**ing**. Modify appropriately for -**ed**, -**er**, -**est**, -**y**, -**s**.)

Prerequisite

■ The children must have investigated and learned the appropriate spelling rules and be able to distinguish long and short vowel phonemes (e.g. /**a**/ and /**ai**/, /**o**/ and /**oa**/).

Resources

For whole-class work

■ 18 cards: three sets of six cards – each set gives six verbs that fit one of the three rules of what we have to do to the verb when adding -**ing**: 1. Nothing, 2. Double the final consonant, 3. Drop the **e** (see 'Practice examples' on page 191)

For independent work

■ Set of verb cards, three for each rule as described above

■ Large sheet of paper with the three columns labelled as above, one per pair or group of three

■ Whiteboards and pens, one per child

Procedure

Whole-class work

1. Draw three numbered columns on the whiteboard corresponding to the three possible actions to take when adding -**ing**: 1. Nothing, 2. Double the final consonant, 3. Drop the **e**.

2. Revise the rules for adding -**ing** to a verb.

3. Explain that this game is a race to see which column will fill up first.

4. Shuffle the verb cards and place them face down in front of you.

5. Show the first card. If there are children in the class who may not understand the word, ask someone to think of a sentence using the word (e.g. **I smile at my cat**).

6. Ask the children to discuss with their talk partners which column the verb belongs in.

7. Ask the children to show the card (or raise the number of fingers) to indicate which column the verb belongs in.

8. If some children show an incorrect card or put the wrong number of fingers up, explore why they made this decision.

9. Place the word in the correct column.

10. Repeat for more verbs. Note which column has filled up first and continue until the next one has filled. Stop the game there.

Independent work

1. The children work in small groups. Each child needs a whiteboard and pen and the group needs a large piece of paper with three columns labelled as above.

2. The verb cards should be placed in a pile, face down in the centre of the table.

3. One child takes a card from the pile and shows it to the group.

4. The children decide which column the word belongs in and try the word on their whiteboards. When all agree, one child records the word in the agreed column on the paper.

5. Another child picks up the next verb card and repeats the process.

Plenary

1. Ask the children to read the words out for each column and check that all groups agree.

2. Ask some children whether there were any words their group disagreed about.

3. If you have looked at adding other endings (e.g. -**ed**, -**y**, -**est**) discuss whether there are similarities or differences between the rules.

Words in words

Purpose

■ To investigate how adding suffixes and prefixes changes words

Use this activity to teach and reinforce prefixes and suffixes.

Prerequisite

■ When you are selecting words for this activity, consider the vocabulary used by the children in your class and select words that they are likely to know. (See also 'Practice examples', page 191.) Explore the function of the prefix or suffix using familiar words, then help to expand the children's vocabulary by asking them to predict meanings of other words with the same prefix or suffix.

Preparation

■ Prepare lists of the words you want to discuss with children and differentiated sets of words for the children to work with in the independent session

Resources

■ Lists of words

■ Whiteboards and pens, one per pair of children

Procedure

1. Show the children two related words, with and without the prefix or suffix. Ask them what they both mean and what has been added to the base word to make the other word. Do the same with three more pairs of words using the same prefix or suffix.

2. Ask the children, in pairs, to make up a sentence for each of two words to share with the class. Draw their attention to the different uses of each of the words.

3. Ask the children to think of other words with the same prefix or suffix and to write the words on their whiteboards. Ask the children to share the words with the class.

4. If it is relevant, show an example in which the spelling of the base word is altered when the suffix is added. Discuss the implications for spelling.

Clap and count

Purpose

■ To provide a routine for spelling long words

Use this activity for spelling compound words, words with prefixes and other multi-syllabic words.

Resources

For whole-class work

■ Differentiated sets of multi-syllable word cards, each card showing one word

■ Whiteboards and pens, one per child

Preparation

For independent work

■ Prepare differentiated sets of word cards (4–12 per group, depending on the children's ability)

Procedure

Whole-class work

1. Say a two-syllable word, clapping the syllables.

2. Do the same with words with three and more syllables including some of the children's names.

3. Point to two children who have names containing a different number of syllables. Clap one of their names and ask the children which one you are clapping.

4. Clap a two-syllable word and draw two lines or boxes on the whiteboard for each syllable.

5. Ask the children to write down the letters for the phonemes in the first syllable and show you.

6. If they are not all correct, take different versions from the children and discuss them.

7. Repeat with the second syllable.

8. Say another word and ask the children to clap it and draw boxes for the number of syllables on their whiteboards and show you.

9. Discuss deviations in the responses.

10. Ask the children to write down the letters for the phonemes in the first syllable and show you.

11. If they are not all correct, take different versions from the children and discuss them.

12. Repeat with the second and subsequent syllables.

13. Summarise the routine, with the children joining in, to help them to remember it: clap and count the syllables, draw the lines, write the letters.

Independent work

1. The children work in groups of up to four to play 'clap and count, draw, write' (as above).

2. Shuffle the word cards and put them in a pile, face down in the centre of the table.

3. When it is their turn, each child should take the top word from the pile, read it aloud and put it face down in front of them.

4. The children go through the same routine: clap and count the syllables, draw the lines, write the letters.

5. The card is then revealed and everybody checks the accuracy of their spelling, awarding themselves 1 point for the correct number of syllables and 1 point for each syllable spelt correctly.

6. Repeat until each child has had at least one turn and then add up the scores to determine the winner.

Plenary

1. Focus on children applying this strategy 'silently' (i.e. without stopping and clapping when trying to work out a spelling).

2. Read out five new words for the children to try and write 'secretly' using the routine: clap and count the syllables, draw the lines, write the letters – but they must not give away the number of syllables. You could show them how to tap very quietly with their fingers.

3. Write up the words and support children in checking their words. What are the difficult bits in each of the words? How does this routine help?

Finding and learning the difficult bits in words

Take it apart and put it back together

Purpose

- To help children learn high-frequency and topic words by developing their ability to identify the potentially difficult element or elements in a word (e.g the double **tt** in **getting**, the unusual spelling of /**oo**/, and the unaccented vowel **i** in **beautiful**).

Resources

- Set of large word cards and blank strips of card (for writing explanation sentences)

- Reusable sticky pads

For independent work

- List of high-frequency or topic words and a list of word descriptions with a blank box beside each description

Procedure

1. Introduce the activity by explaining that if we understand why a word is spelt in a particular way, it can help us to remember how to spell that word accurately when we are writing.

2. Write a word on the whiteboard. Ask the children why they think it is spelt like this. Allow some thinking time and then take feedback.

3. Follow the sequence below to 'take the word apart and put it back together again'.

- The children say the word out loud and clap the syllables – underline these on the whiteboard.

- The children count the phonemes and hold up the correct number of fingers. Draw in sound buttons on the whiteboard.

- The children spot any other distinctive features – note these and/or highlight the particular part of the word.

- Summarise all the features in a description: the children suggest a sentence orally, you select succinct and accurate ideas and write a description on a strip of card (e.g. **their**: this word has one syllable, two phonemes and it begins with the letters **the** just like two related words **them** and **they**; **wanted**: this verb has two syllables, six phonemes, it begins with the 'w special' (see page 187) and has an -**ed** ending for the past tense).

4. Continue with more words so that children get used to the routine.

5. Check the children's understanding of the descriptions. Give some children the sentence strips and some the cards with the words you have described. Ask them to read their cards.

6. Choose a child to bring a sentence strip out and stick it on the whiteboard. Read the description together and ask the child who has the correct word card to bring it to the whiteboard. The first child checks the word and sticks it on the whiteboard if it matches the description. The other children put their thumbs up or down to show whether they agree or not. Repeat until all the sentences are matched with words.

Plenary

1. Ask a child to describe a word. (It could be a word on the list or another word entirely.) Can any of the other children find a word that matches the description?

2. Talk about how this activity can help the children to learn particular spellings. They have taken words apart and looked at distinctive features. This will help them to remember the spellings. Ask each child to choose one word from the list and write it, with the description, in their spelling log. Challenge them to learn it. When they do independent writing they can expect to see an improvement in the spelling of this word.

Learning and practising spellings

Memory strategies

Purpose

■ To develop familiarity with different strategies for memorising high-frequency or topic words

Resources

■ Poster of four memory strategies (see next page)

■ List of words to be spelt

Procedure

Whole-class work

1. Introduce the activity by explaining that in addition to knowing how a word is constructed we may need additional aids to memory.

2. Display the poster of four memory strategies and tell the children that it contains three good ideas for helping them to remember spellings, and a final emergency idea (in case nothing else works).

3. Write a word on the whiteboard, ask the children to read it together and clap the syllables.

4. Discuss with the children the features of the word that might make it difficult to remember and which memory strategy might be helpful.

5. Rub the word off the whiteboard and ask the children to write the word.

6. If children made errors, discuss them in relation to the memory strategy.

7. Repeat 3–6 with another word.

8. Write another word on the whiteboard, ask the children to read it and clap the syllables.

9. Ask the children to discuss with their partners which memory strategy they could use, then ask them to learn the word.

10. Rub the word off the whiteboard and ask the children to write the word.

11. Discuss the strategies chosen and their effectiveness for learning the word.

12. Repeat 8–11 with two more words.

13. Finally dictate each word learned during the lesson for the children to write.

Strategies	Explanations
1. Syllables	To learn my word I can listen to how many syllables there are so I can break it into smaller bits to remember (e.g. **Sep-tem-ber**, **ba-by**)
2. Base words	To learn my word I can find its base word (e.g. Smiling – base smile +**ing**, e.g. women = **wo** + men)
3. Analogy	To learn my word I can use words that I already know to help me (e.g. could: would, should)
4. Mnemonics	To learn my word I can make up a sentence to help me remember it (e.g. could – O U Lucky Duck; people – people eat orange peel like elephants)

Learning words

The best way of giving children words to memorise is to provide a sentence for children to learn so that they get used to using the target words in context. The sentences could be practised at home (or in time allocated during the school day) and then children can show what they have learned by writing the sentences at the beginning of spelling sessions.

The purpose of the following two routines is for children to:

- show what they have learned;

- practise writing words that follow the same pattern or convention;

- use the words in the context of a sentence;

- reflect on what they have learned and learn from their errors.

The children are involved in assessing their own learning as they check their work. They are encouraged to explain their decisions about spelling so that they can understand their success and overcome misconceptions. They use their spelling logs to record words that they often have difficulty with.

Routine A

Preparation

- Select words and devise a sentence for dictation. Write out a list of all the words to be used in the routine, and the final sentence.

Resources

- Sentence for dictation

- List of words

Procedure

Routine A is made up of the following five elements.

1. **Show me what you know.** Test the children on the words they have been learning. Either read the whole sentence and ask them to write it, or read the individual target words.

2. **Spell the word.** Select five more words that follow the same pattern or convention. Remind the children about the convention or spelling pattern they explored. Explain that they will be able to use what they have learned to try spelling the new words.

3. **Read out one word at a time.** All the children write it, read what they have written and check that they are happy with it.

4. **Write the sentence.** Dictate a sentence that includes several target words. Break it into meaningful chunks, repeating each string of words several times. Give children time to check what they have written and remind them of the target features (e.g. **-ed** endings; different spellings of the long vowel phoneme, strategy for remembering a difficult bit).

5. **What have I learned?** Display the list of words for children to use when they are checking their own work. They work in pairs supporting one another in identifying correct spellings and underlining any errors.

Focus on successful strategies, asking what the children have learned that has helped them spell this word correctly. Encourage the children to articulate what they know and how they have applied it. Then focus on some errors and help children to understand why they might have mis-spelt the word – were they tripped up by the difficult bit? Did they forget to apply the rule?

Routine B

Preparation

■ Devise two sentences that include examples of words from this phase and incorporate words from previous phases. Select three words for the children to make into their own sentences. Write out the dictations, and the words as three word cards.

For this activity the children should write their sentences in a notebook so that there is an ongoing record of their progress.

Resources

■ Two sentences

■ Three word cards

Procedure

Routine B is made up of the following three elements.

1. **Write the sentence.** Dictate two sentences that include target words and other words needing reinforcement. Break each sentence into meaningful chunks, repeating each string of words several times. Give children time to check what they have written and ask them to look out for words they have been working on. Is there a pattern to follow or a rule to apply?

2. **Create a new sentence.** Read out the three words you have chosen and provide children with a theme, e.g. create a new sentence about children eating lunch using the words **wanted**, **their** and **shared**. Give the children time to write their sentences, read through and check them. Have they used the strategies they have been learning to recall the correct spelling?

One (confident) child could write his sentence 'in secret' on the whiteboard. Reveal this sentence and ask the children to read it through. Ask which words are spelt correctly. Analyse any errors and talk about why they might have been made.

3. **What have I learned?** Display the sentences from the earlier dictation and word cards for the new sentences. Ask children to check their work in pairs. They support one another in identifying correct spellings and underlining any errors.

Possible questions are: *Were there words in this dictation that you have mis-spelt before? Did you get them right this time? What strategy did you use to remember the difficult bit? Did you spell the target words correctly in your sentence?* Give the children the opportunity to select one or two words to add to their spelling logs.

These are likely to be words that they use regularly and find difficult to spell.

For really tricky words the following process – simultaneous oral spelling – has proved useful for children.

Procedure

1. The children copy out word to be learned on a card.

2. They read it aloud then turn the card over.

3. Ask them to write out the word, naming each letter as they write it.

4. They read aloud the word they have written.

5. Then ask them to turn the card over and compare their spelling with the correct spelling.

6. Repeat 2–5 three times.

Do this for six consecutive days.

Application of spelling in writing

Children's growing understanding of why words are spelt in a particular way is valuable only if they go on to apply it in their independent writing. Children should be able to spell an ever-increasing number of words accurately and to check and correct their own work. This process is supported through:

■ shared writing: the teacher demonstrates how to apply spelling strategies while writing and teaches proofreading skills;

■ guided and independent writing: the children apply what they have been taught. This is the opportunity to think about the whole writing process: composition as well as spelling, handwriting and punctuation;

- marking the children's work: the teacher can assess their progress and their ability to understand and apply what has been taught, then identify targets for further improvement;

- teaching and practising handwriting: learning and practising a fluent joined style will support the children's spelling development.

Marking

Marking provides the opportunity to see how well individual children understand and apply what has been taught and should always relate to the specific focus for teaching.

- Set clear expectations when the children start to write. Remind them of the strategies, rules and conventions that they can apply. Expectations and marking will reflect the children's cumulative knowledge but the marking should not go beyond what has been taught about spelling. Ensure that the children know what the criteria for success are in this particular piece of work. For example: *Now that you understand the rules for adding -**ed** to regular verbs I will expect you to spell these words correctly.*

- Analyse children's errors. Look closely at the strategies the children are using. What does this tell you about their understanding? For example, a child using **jumpt** instead of **jumped** is using phonological knowledge but does not yet understand about adding -**ed** to verbs in the past tense.

- Provide feedback and time to respond. In your comments to the children, focus on a limited number of spelling errors that relate to a particular letter string or spelling convention. Ensure that the children have had time to read or discuss your feedback and clarify expectations about what they should do next.

- Set mini-targets. Present expectations for independent spelling in terms of simple targets that will apply to all the writing the children do. These targets would generally be differentiated for groups, but it may be appropriate to tailor a target to include specific 'problem' words for an individual (e.g. I expect to spell these words correctly in all my writing: **said, they**).

Targets can be written into spelling logs for the children to refer to regularly.

Children gaining independence

- Strategies for spelling during writing. Children need strategies to help them attempt spellings they are not sure of as they are writing, without interrupting the flow of their composition. Aim to build up routines where the children will try different strategies before asking for help (see the poster 'Things to do before asking someone' on page 192).

- Using spelling logs. Children can each have a log – ideally in the form of a loose-leaf folder that can be added to – to record the particular spellings they need to focus on in their work. The spelling log can be used in the following two main ways.

  1. As part of the spelling programme: a regular part of the spelling activities involves the children identifying specific words that they need to continue to work on. These could be words exemplifying a particular pattern or convention or high-frequency words. These words are put into the children's logs with tips on how to remember the spelling.

  2. To record spellings arising from each child's independent writing: these words will be specific to the individual child and will be those that frequently trip them up as they are writing. These words can be identified as part of the proofreading process and children can be involved in devising strategies for learning them and monitoring whether they spell the target words correctly in subsequent work.

The children should have no more than five target words at a time and these should be reviewed at intervals (e.g. each half-term). The children can look for evidence of correct spellings in their independent writing and remove the word from the list once it has been spelt correctly five times in a row. The teacher can write the child's spelling target into the log so that the child can refer to it regularly.

Proofreading

Children need to be taught how to proofread their work as part of the writing process. Editing for spelling (or typographic errors) should take place after the writer is satisfied with all other elements of the writing. It is important that teachers model the proofreading process in shared writing.

1. Preparation. Towards the end of a unit of work, after the children have revisited and revised their work in terms of structure and content, sentence construction and punctuation, the teacher selects an example of one child's work, writes it out and makes a few changes so that it is not immediately recognisable.

2. Shared writing. Read through the work as the children follow, explaining that you are looking for a particular type of spelling error, related to specific recent teaching focuses (e.g. the spelling of -**ed** endings). Think aloud as you identify each error and encourage the children to go through the following routine.

   - Underline the part of the word that looks wrong and explain why it looks wrong.

   - Try out an alternative spelling.

- Ask yourself whether it looks right.

- Check from another source (e.g. words around the room, another child, spelling log, dictionary).

- Write in the correct spelling.

Repeat this until the target words have been corrected. Are there any patterns in these errors? Is there a strategy that would help the children to avoid the same errors in the future (e.g. consonant doubling after short vowels)?

3. Independent and guided writing. The children repeat the same process for their own writing across the curriculum. Less confident writers can be supported in this process with guided writing sessions.

Using dictionaries and spelling checkers

Children should be taught to use a dictionary to check their spelling. By Phase Six, the repeated singing of an alphabet song at earlier phases should have familiarised them with alphabetical order. Their first dictionary practice should be with words starting with different letters, but once they are competent at this, they should learn how to look at second and subsequent letters when necessary, learning, for example, that words starting **al**- come before words starting **an**- and **as**-, and words starting **ben**- come before words starting **ber**-. Knowledge gained in Phase Five of different ways of spelling particular sounds is also relevant in dictionary use: for example a child who tries to look up believe under **belee**- needs to be reminded to look under other possible spellings of the /**ee**/ sound. Having found the correct spelling of a word, children should be encouraged to memorise it.

Unless a first attempt at spelling a word is logical and reasonably close to the target, a spelling checker may suggest words which are not the one required. Children need to be taught not just to accept these suggestions, but to sound them out carefully to double-check whether the pronunciation matches that of the word they are trying to spell.

Links with handwriting

Developing a fluent joined style is an important part of learning to spell and the teaching of spelling and handwriting should be closely linked.

- Handwriting sessions. As children are taught the basic joins they can practise joining each digraph as one unit. This can develop into practising letter strings and complete words linked to the specific focus for teaching (e.g. joining **w**-**a** to support work on the 'w special' – see page 187).

- High-frequency words can be demonstrated and practised as joined units (e.g. the, was, said).

- Spelling sessions. The children need to see the target words written in joined script as frequently as possible and to practise writing words, for example in dictations and at home using joined script themselves.

Knowledge of the spelling system

In Phase Six children need to acquire more word-specific knowledge. They still need to segment words into phonemes to spell them, but they also learn that good spelling involves not only doing this and representing all the phonemes plausibly but also, where necessary, choosing the right grapheme from several possibilities.

In some cases, word-specific spellings (e.g. sea/see; goal/pole/bowl/soul; zoo/clue/flew/you) simply have to be learned. It is important to devote time in this phase to learning common words with rare or irregular spellings (e.g. they, there, said) as the quantity children write increases and without correction they may practise incorrect spellings that are later difficult to put right.

However, there are spelling conventions or guidelines that generalise across many words and that children should understand. Where there are exceptions these can usually be dealt with as they arise in children's reading and writing.

Some useful spelling guidelines

1. The position of a phoneme in a word may rule out certain graphemes for that phoneme. The **ai** and **oi** spellings do not occur at the end of English words or immediately before suffixes; instead, the **ay** and **oy** spellings are used in these positions (e.g. play, played, playing, playful, joy, joyful, enjoying, enjoyment). In other positions, the /ai/ sound is most often spelled **ai** or **a**-consonant-vowel, as in rain, date and bacon. The same principle applies in choosing between **oi** and **oy**: **oy** is used at the end of a word or immediately before a suffix, and **oi** is used elsewhere. There is no other spelling for this phoneme.

Note that it is recommended that teachers should (at least at first) simply pronounce the relevant vowel sounds for the children – /a/, /e/, /i/, /o/ and /u/; /ai/, /ee/, /igh/, /oa/ and /oo/. Later the terms 'long' and 'short' can be useful when children need to form more general concepts about spelling patterns.

2. When an /o/ sound follows a /**w**/ sound, it is frequently spelt with the letter **a** (e.g. was, wallet, want, wash, watch, wander) – often known as the 'w special'. This extends to many words where the /**w**/ sound comes from the **qu** grapheme (e.g. quarrel, quantity, squad, squash).

3. When an /**ur**/ sound follows the letter **w** (but not **qu**) it is usually spelt **or** (e.g. word, worm, work, worship, worth). The important exception is were.

4. An /**or**/ sound before an /**l**/ sound is frequently spelled with the letter /**a**/ (e.g. all, ball, call, always).

5. English words do not end in the letter **v** unless they are abbreviations (e.g. rev). If a word ends in a /v/ sound, **e** must be added after the **v** in the spelling (e.g. give, have, live, love, above). This may seem confusing, because it suggests that the vowels should have their 'long' sounds (as in alive, save and stove) but in fact there are very few words in the give/have category (i.e. words with 'short' vowels) – they are mostly common words and are quickly learned.

6. Elisions, sometimes known as contractions, such as I'm, let's and can't are usually easy to spell, but children need to know where to put the apostrophe. They should be taught that it marks the place where letters are omitted.

7. Confusions are common between their and there and can persist unless appropriate teaching is given. There is related in meaning and spelling to here and where; all are concerned with place. Their is related in meaning (plural person) and spelling to they and them. To avoid confusing children, experience shows it is advisable not to teach these two similar sounding words there and their at the same time but to secure the understanding of one of them before teaching the other.

   An additional problem with the word their is its unusual letter order. However, if children know that they, them and their share the same first three letters, they are less likely to misspell their as thier.

8. Giving vowel graphemes their full value in reading can help with the spelling of the schwa sound. For example, if children at first sound out the word important in their reading with a clear /a/ sound in the last syllable, this will help them to remember to spell the **schwa** sound in that syllable with the letter **a** rather than with any other vowel letter.

9. In deciding whether to use **ant** or **ent**, **ance** or **ence** at the end of a word, it is often helpful to consider whether there is a related word where the vowel sound is more clearly pronounced. When deciding, for example, between occupant or occupent the related word occupation shows that the vowel letter must be **a**. Similarly, if one is unsure about residance or residence, the word residential shows that the letter must be **e**.

Note: The **i** before **e** except after **c** rule is not worth teaching. It applies only to words in which the **ie** or **ei** stands for a clear /ee/ sound and unless this is known, words such as sufficient, veil and their look like exceptions. There are so few words where the **ei** spelling for the /ee/ sound follows the letter **c** that it is easier to learn the specific words: receive, conceive, deceive (+ the related words receipt, conceit, deceit), perceive and ceiling.

Adding suffixes to words

During Phase Six, children should also start to learn spelling conventions for adding common endings (suffixes) to words. Most children will have taken words with suffixes in their stride in reading, but for spelling purposes they now need more systematic teaching both of the suffixes themselves and of how the spelling of base words may have to change slightly when suffixes are added. Some grammatical awareness is also helpful here: just knowing that the regular past tense ending is spelt -**ed** is not enough – children also need to be aware that the word they are trying to spell is a past tense word. Without this awareness, they may, for example, spell **hopped** as **hopt**, **played** as **plaid**, **grabbed** as **grabd** and **started** as **startid** – perfectly accurate phonemically, but not correct. Conversely, once they have understood that the -**ed** ending can sometimes sound like /**t**/, they may try to spell **soft** as **soffed**, unless they realise that this word is not the past tense of a verb. (See 'Introducing and teaching the past tense' on page 170).

These are examples of common suffixes suitable for Phase Six:

- **-s** and **-es**: added to nouns and verbs, as in **cats**, **runs**, **bushes**, **catches**;

- **-ed** and -**ing**: added to verbs, as in **hopped**, **hopping**, **hoped**, **hoping**;

- **-ful**: added to nouns, as in **careful**, **painful**, **playful**, **restful**, **mouthful**;

- **-er**: added to verbs to denote the person doing the action and to adjectives to give the comparative form, as in **runner**, **reader**, **writer**, **bigger**, **slower**;

- **-est**: added to adjectives, as in **biggest**, **slowest**, **happiest**, **latest**;

- **-ly**: added to adjectives to form adverbs, as in **sadly**, **happily**, **brightly**, **lately**;

- **-ment**: added to verbs to form nouns, as in **payment**, **advertisement**, **development**;

- **-ness**: added to adjectives to form nouns, as in **darkness**, **happiness**, **sadness**;

- **-y**: added to nouns to form adjectives, as in **funny**, **smoky**, **sandy**.

The spelling of a suffix is always the same, except in the case of -**s** and -**es**.

Adding -s and -es to nouns and verbs

Generally, -**s** is simply added to the base word. The suffix -**es** is used after words ending in s(**s**), **ch**, **sh** and z(**z**), and when **y** is replaced by **i**. Examples include **buses**, **passes**, **benches**, **catches**, **rushes**, **buzzes**, **babies**. (In words such as **buses**, **passes**, **benches** and **catches**, the extra syllable is easy to hear and helps with the spelling.) Words such as **knife**, **leaf** and **loaf** become **knives**, **leaves** and **loaves** and again the change in spelling is obvious from the change in the pronunciation of the words.

Adding other suffixes

Other suffixes have just one spelling. As with **-s** and **-es**, many can be added to base words without affecting the spelling of the base word. Adding a suffix may sometimes mean, however, that the last letter of the base word needs to be dropped, changed or doubled, and there are guidelines for this. Once children know the guidelines, they can apply them to many different words. Only three kinds of base words may need their last letters to be changed – those ending in:

- an -**e** that is part of a split digraph (e.g. **hope**, **safe**, **use**);

- a -**y** preceded by a consonant (e.g. **happy**, **baby**, **carry**);

- a single consonant letter preceded by a single vowel letter (e.g. **hop**, **red**, **run**). This simplified version of the guideline applies reliably to single-syllable words. Later, children will need to learn that in words of more than one syllable, stress also needs to be taken into account.

General guidelines for adding other suffixes

Children should be taught to think in terms of base words and suffixes whenever appropriate. Suffixes are easily learned and many base words will already be familiar from Phases Two to Five.

1. If a base word ends in an **e** which is part of a split digraph, drop the **e** if the suffix begins with a vowel (e.g. **hope** – **hoping**; **like** – **liked**: the **e** before the **d** is part of the suffix, not part of the base word). Keep the **e** if the suffix begins with a consonant (e.g. **hope** – **hopeful**; **safe** – **safely**).

2. If a base word ends in **y** preceded by a consonant, change the **y** to **i** before all suffixes except those beginning with **i** (e.g. **happy** – **happiness**, **happier**; **baby** – **babies**; **carry** – **carried**). Keep the **y** if the suffix begins with **i**, not permissible in English (e.g. **baby** – **babyish**; **carry** – **carrying**), as **ii** is not permissible in English except in **taxiing** and **skiing**.

3. If a base word ends in a single consonant letter preceded by a single vowel letter and the suffix begins with a vowel, double the consonant letter. Another way of stating this guideline is that there need to be two consonant letters between a 'short' vowel (vowel sounds learned in Phase Two – see also the note on page 187) and a suffix beginning with a vowel (e.g. **hop** – **hopped**, **hopping**; **red** – **redder**, **reddest**; **run** – **running**, **runner**).

In all other cases, the suffix can simply be added without any change being made to the spelling of the base word. This means that for words in 1 and 3 above, the spelling of the base word does not change if a suffix beginning with a consonant is added (e.g. **lame** + **ness** = **lameness**; **glad** + **ly** = **gladly**). Similarly, no change occurs if the base word ends in any way other than those mentioned in 1, 2 and 3 above.

Practice examples

Examples for practising adding the suffixes -s or -es		
stop	fizz	hurry
park	circus	fly
bunch	room	bunny
mend	fuss	marry
dish	goal	dry
thank	cross	curry
crash	boat	cry
match	buzz	puppy
bark	melt	try
night	stitch	fry

Examples for practising adding the suffixes -ing, -ed, -s, -er, -est, -y, -en

All the base words need changes made before the suffixes are added.

Words ending in -e	Words ending in -y	Words ending in a single consonant
like (ing)	marry (ed)	stop (ing)
ride (er)	funny (er)	mad (er)
tame (est)	worry (ed)	skip (ed)
bone (y)	copy (er)	run (ing)
bake (ed)	hurry (ed)	hop (er)
hike (ing)	messy (est)	nod (ed)
fine (est)	lucky (er)	pad (ing)
wave (ed)	ferry (s)	hid (en)
rule (er)	carry (ed)	hot (est)
rude (est)	pony (s)	rip (ed)

Examples for practising adding the suffixes -ing, -ed, -ful, -ly, -est, -er, -ment, -ness, -en

Some of the base words need to be changed before the suffixes are added but some do not.

Remember: a final **e** in the base word may or may not need to be dropped	Remember: a final **y** in the base word may or may not need to be changed to **i**	Remember: a final consonant in the base word may or may not need to be double.
spite (ful)	merry (ly)	bad (ly)
rude (ly)	employ (ment)	flap (ed)
white (er)	play (ed)	send (ing)
bite (ing)	enjoy (ment)	slim (est)
lame (ness)	silly (ness)	fan (ed)
safe (ly)	funny (est)	sad (ness)
amuse (ment)	obey (ing)	put (ing)
rise (ing)	sunny (er)	flat (en)
time (ed)	happy (ly)	bat (ing)
use (ful)	stay (ed)	dark (est)

Things to do before asking someone

What can I do if I get stuck on a spelling?

Find another word that will do for now and come back to this one later or even leave a gap.

Or try these three things before you ask someone:

1. Try using phonic strategies. Say the word and segment the phonemes. Split a long word into syllables.

2. Think about other words that sound the same. Can you use what you know about spelling similar words?

3. Look at your spelling log, word banks or displays in the classroom. Can you find the word you want? Try looking for the word in a dictionary.

Appendix 1

100 high-frequency words in order				
1. the	21. that	41. not	61. look	81. put
2. and	22. with	42. then	62. don't	82. could
3. a	23. all	43. were	63. come	83. house
4. to	24. we	44. go	64. will	84. old
5. said	25. can	45. little	65. into	85. too
6. in	26. are	46. as	66. back	86. by
7. he	27. up	47. no	67. from	87. day
8. I	28. had	48. mum	68. children	88. made
9. of	29. my	49. one	69. him	89. time
10. it	30. her	50. them	70. Mr	90. I'm
11. was	31. what	51. do	71. get	91. if
12. you	32. there	52. me	72. just	92. help
13. they	33. out	53. down	73. now	93. Mrs
14. on	34. this	54. dad	74. came	94. called
15. she	35. have	55. big	75. oh	95. here
16. is	36. went	56. when	76. about	96. off
17. for	37. be	57. it's	77. got	97. asked
18. at	38. like	58. see	78. their	98. saw
19. his	39. some	59. looked	79. people	99. make
20. but	40. so	60. very	80. your	100. an

Tables from: Masterson, J., Stuart, M., Dixon, M. and Lovejoy, S. (2003) Children's Printed Word Database: Economic and Social Research Council funded project, R00023406

100 high-frequency words in phases

Phase Two

Decodable words		Tricky words
a	had	the
an	back	to
as	and	I
at	get	no
if	big	go
in	him	into
is	his	
it	not	
of	got	
off	up	
on	mum	
can	but	
dad	put (*north*)	

100 high-frequency words in phases

Phase Three

Decodable words		Tricky words	
will	see	he	you
that	for	she	they
this	now	we	all
then	down	me	are
them	look	be	my
with	too	was	her

100 high-frequency words in phases

Phase Four

Decodable words		Tricky words	
went		said	were
it's		have	there
from		like	little
children		so	one
just		do	when
help		some	out
		come	what

100 high-frequency words in phases

Phase Five

Note that some of the words that were tricky in earlier phases become fully decodable in Phase Five

Decodable words		Tricky words
don't	day	oh
old	made	their
I'm	came	people
by	make	Mr
time	here	Mrs
	saw	looked
house	very	called
about	put (*south*)	asked
your		could

Next 200 common words in order of frequency

This list is read down columns (i.e in the list, **water** is the most frequently used and **grow** is the least frequently used)

water	other	fast	air	use
away	food	only	trees	along
good	fox	many	bad	plants
want	through	laughed	tea	dragon
over	way	let's	top	pulled
how	been	much	eyes	we're
did	stop	suddenly	fell	fly
man	must	told	friends	grow
going	red	another	box	
where	door	great	dark	
would	right	why	grandad	
or	sea	cried	there's	
took	these	keep	looking	
school	began	room	end	
think	boy	last	than	
home	animals	jumped	best	
who	never	because	better	
didn't	next	even	hot	
ran	first	am	sun	
know	work	before	across	
bear	lots	gran	gone	
can't	need	clothes	hard	
again	that's	tell	floppy	
cat	baby	key	really	
long	fish	fun	wind	
things	gave	place	wish	
new	mouse	mother	eggs	
after	something	sat	once	
wanted	bed	boat	please	
eat	may	window	thing	
everyone	still	sleep	stopped	
our	found	feet	ever	
two	live	morning	miss	
has	say	queen	most	
yes	soon	each	cold	
play	night	book	park	
take	narrator	its	lived	
thought	small	green	birds	
dog	car	different	duck	
well	couldn't	let	horse	
find	three	girl	rabbit	
more	head	which	white	
I'll	king	inside	coming	
round	town	run	he's	
tree	I've	any	river	
magic	around	under	liked	
shouted	every	hat	giant	
us	garden	snow	looks	

Tables from: Masterson, J., Stuart, M., Dixon, M. and Lovejoy, S. (2003) Children's Printed Word Database: Economic and Social Research Coucil funded project, R00023406

Appendix 2

Letter formation

Appendix 3

Assessment

Progress check for each phase

Phase 1

By the end of phase 1 children will have experienced a wealth of listening activities including songs, stories and rhymes. They will be able to distinguish between speech sounds and many will be able to blend and segment words orally. Some will also be able to recognise spoken words that rhyme and will be able to provide a string of rhyming words, but inability to do this does not prevent moving on to Phase Two as these speaking and listening activities continue.

Phase Two (up to 6 weeks)

By the end of Phase Two children should:

- give the sound when shown any Phase Two letter, securing first the starter letters **s**, **a**, **t**, **p**, **i**, **n**;
- find any Phase Two letter, from a display, when given the sound;
- be able to orally blend and segment CVC words;
- be able to blend and segment in order to read and spell (using magnetic letters) VC words such as: **if**, **am**, **on**, **up** and 'silly names' such as **ip**, **ug** and **ock**;
- be able to read the five tricky words **the**, **to**, **I**, **no**, **go**.

Phase Three (up to 12 weeks)

By the end of Phase Three children should:

- give the sound when shown all or most Phase Two and Phase Three graphemes;
- find all or most Phase Two and Phase Three graphemes, from a display, when given the sound;
- be able to blend and read CVC words (i.e. single-syllable words consisting of Phase Two and Phase Three graphemes);
- be able to segment and make a phonemically plausible attempt at spelling CVC words (i.e. single-syllable words consisting of Phase Two and Phase Three graphemes);
- be able to read the tricky words **he**, **she**, **we**, **me**, **be**, **was**, **my**, **you**, **her**, **they**, **all**, **are**;
- be able to spell the tricky words **the**, **to**, **I**, **no**, **go**;
- write each letter correctly when following a model.

Phase Four (4–6 weeks)

By the end of Phase Four children should:

- give the sound when shown any Phase Two and Phase Three grapheme;
- find any Phase Two and Phase Three grapheme, from a display, when given the sound;
- be able to blend and read words containing adjacent consonants;
- be able to segment and spell words containing adjacent consonants;
- be able to read the tricky words some, one, said, come, do, so, were, when, have, there, out, like, little, what;
- be able to spell the tricky words he, she, we, me, be, was, my, you, her, they, all, are;
- write each letter, usually correctly.

Phase Five (throughout Year 1)

By the end of Phase Five children should:

- give the sound when shown any grapheme that has been taught;
- for any given sound, write the common graphemes;
- apply phonic knowledge and skill as the prime approach to reading and spelling unfamiliar words that are not completely decodable;
- read and spell phonically decodable two-syllable and three-syllable words;
- read automatically all the words in the list of 100 high-frequency words;
- accurately spell most of the words in the list of 100 high-frequency words;
- form each letter correctly.

Assessment tasks

(See the section on assessment in the *Notes of Guidance for Practitioners and Teachers*, page 16.)

Contents

- Grapheme–phoneme correspondences task

- Oral blending task

- Oral segmentation task

- Non-word reading task

Grapheme–phoneme correspondences task

s, a, t, p, i, n

Securing success from the start for all beginner readers is an obvious but crucially important aim of the Letters and Sounds programme. The first six letters children will learn to read and write at the start of the systematic teaching of phonics in Phase Two are s, a, t, p, i, n. Once learned, these letters provide children with an easy, but very useful, set of phoneme–grapheme correspondences with which to build two-letter and three-letter words.

Purpose

- To assess knowledge of grapheme–phoneme correspondences

Resources

- Grapheme card (see the example below)

- Group assessment sheet with the names of the children entered (see the example on page 201–202)

Procedure

1. Display the grapheme card.

2. For each correct letter, record the date of assessment on the group assessment sheet.

Example grapheme cards

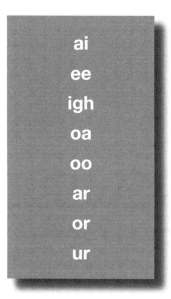

00281-2007BKT-EN

Example group assessment sheet for grapheme–phoneme correspondences

Phase Two

Name of child														
s														
a														
t														
p														
i														
n														
m														
d														
g														
o														
c														
k														
ck														
e														
u														
r														
h														
b														
f, ff														
l, ll														
ss														

Phase Three

Name of child														
j														
v														
w														
x														
y														
z, zz														
qu														
ch														
sh														
th, th														
ng														
ai														
ee														
igh														
oa														
oo, oo														
ar														
or														
ur														
ow														
oi														
ear														
air														
ure														
er														

00281-2007BK i-EN
© Crown copyright 2007

Oral blending task

Purpose

- To assess oral blending

Resources

- Sheet displaying all the pictures of the words to be blended (optional, see 7 below)

- Assessment response sheet for each child (see the example on page 204)

Procedure

1. Use the practice items (see below) to explain the task to the child as follows: *We're going to play a listening game. I'm going to speak like a robot. I want you to listen carefully and tell me the word I'm trying to say. Let's practise. The word is c - a - t. What is the robot trying to say?*

2. If the child needs more prompting, say: *It's a word you know. Listen again.*

3. Proceed with the assessment items.

4. Offer each word in turn, leaving just less than a one-second interval between phonemes and record the child's first response.

5. Discontinue after three consecutive errors.

6. Praise the child, whether successful or not, for a positive attitude or disposition to the task – for example for 'having a go' at a difficult job, sitting still and listening, taking time to think – and comment that good learners do those things.

7. Rather than ask the child to say the word, you could ask the child to point to the correct picture.

Practice items: c - a - t   m - u - m

Name Word to be spoken by the adult	Record response. Tick if correct. If incorrect, record exactly what the child said or did
1. m - a - n	
2. s - o - ck	
3. c - u - p	
4. p - e - g	
5. f - i - sh	
6. h - a - n - d	
7. t - e - n - t	
8. f - l - a - g	
9. s - p - oo - n	
10. s - t - a - m - p	

Oral segmentation task

Oral segmentation of words into three phonemes and four phonemes.

Purpose

- To assess oral segmentation

Resources

- Assessment response sheet for each child (see example)

Procedure

1. Use the practice items (see below) to explain the task to the child:

   Now it's your turn to speak like a robot. I'm going to say a word and I want you to say all the sounds in the word, just like I did in the last game. Let's practise. The word is 'cat'. This is how the robot says cat, c-a-t. You do it.

   Instead of saying zip, the robot says z-i-p. How does the robot say mum?

2. Provide the correct response if the child responds incorrectly.

3. Proceed with the assessment items.

4. Offer each word in turn and record the child's first response.

5. Discontinue after three consecutive errors.

6. Praise the child, whether successful or not, for a positive attitude or disposition to the task – for example for 'having a go' at a difficult job, sitting still and listening, taking time to think – and comment that good learners do those things.

Practice items: cat, zip, mum

Name Word to be spoken by the adult	Record the child's response. Tick, if correct. If incorrect, record exactly what the child said or did.
1. jam	
2. zip	
3. net	
4. dog	
5. mint	
6. sand	
7. gran	
8. snack	
9. crash	
10. dress	

Non-word reading task

Purpose

- To assess grapheme recognition

- To assess blending

Resources

- Non-words on a shopping list

- Assessment response sheet for each child (see the example on page 207)

Procedure

1. Use a scenario to put this task in a context for the child, for example a friendly alien came to earth in a space ship. The alien had lists of things to take back to his own planet. This is what was written on the alien's first list, second list, etc.

2. Say: *Can you to read the words. Do you think you would be able to help the alien find the things on the list?*

3. Ask the child to say the sound for each grapheme and then to blend them to make a 'word'.

4. Record the sound for each grapheme and the blended word (see the example response sheet on page 207).

5. Stop after three consecutive errors.

Phase 2

og	pim	reb	cag
ab	ket	nud	meck
liss	hin		

Phase 3

dar	veng	gax	chee
zort	jigh	hish	yurk
sair	quoam	koob	waiber
kear	doit	fowd	thorden

Phase 4

plood	dreet	skarb	kelf
grint	bamp	shreb	pronk
theest	fowsping	spunch	glorpid

Example response sheet for non-word reading task at Phase Two

Name	Graphemes (e.g. o-g)	Reading (e.g. og)
og		
ab		
liss		
pim		
ket		
hin		
reb		
nud		
cag		
meck		

Acknowledgements

Activities based directly on Looking and Listening Pack. © Heywood Middleton & Rochdale Primary Care Trust. Used with kind permission.

Tables entitled '100 high-frequency words in order', and 'Next 200 common words in order of frequency' from Masterson, J., Stuart, M., Dixon, M. & Lovejoy, S. (2003) Children's Printed Word Database. Economic and Social Research Council funded project, R00023406. Used with kind permission.

Special thanks are due to ICAN for their contribution to Phase One.